THE CATTLEYAS
AND THEIR RELATIVES

Volume II. The Laelias

Fig. 1. *Laelia speciosa.* Type species for the genus *Laelia.* Plate from James Bateman's *The Orchidaceae of Mexico and Guatemala,* 1837–1843, as *L. majalis.*

THE CATTLEYAS
AND THEIR RELATIVES

Volume II. The Laelias

A book in six parts
by

CARL L. WITHNER

TIMBER PRESS
Portland, Oregon

ISBN 0-88192-161-0
Printed in Hong Kong

TIMBER PRESS, INC.
9999 S.W. Wilshire
Portland, Oregon 97225

Library of Congress Cataloging-in-Publication Data

(Revised for vol. II)

Withner, Carl L. (Carl Leslie)
   The Cattleyas and their relatives.

   Includes bibliographical references and indexes.
   Contents: v. 1. The Cattleyas -- The Laelias.
   1. Orchids. 2. Cattleyas. 3. Orchid culture.
4. Orchids--Latin America. I. Title.
SB409.W793 1988   635.9'3415   88-8560
ISBN 0-88192-099-1 (v. 1)

Table of Contents

This volume is dedicated
to Pat,
my understanding wife and best
companion.
She has generously shared me with
the orchids for 48 years.

Preface

Getting this material on the laelias together has become more and more like a detective story. The laelias are not as well known as the cattleyas (Volume I of this series), and many have been described only in the last 10–15 years. Some are just recently finding their way into cultivation in their native country (Brazil), and we have just not seen them often enough to be familiar with their names and clonal variations. Little has been written about most of the new species, and they have often been confused and misidentified in our collections. Going back to the original descriptions involves finding a number of obscure or old publications, and that in itself requires considerable searching. Dr. Phillip Cribb, at Kew Gardens in England, has kindly helped me obtain certain pages not readily found in North America.

In the case of *Laelia elegans,* a natural hybrid popular under a variety of names in the latter part of the last century, what was once a well recognized and readily available plant is no longer to be found. It should probably be rehybridized from selected parents in cultivation. After we have dealt with all of the new *Laelia* names for as many years as we have the cattleya epithets, no doubt they will come as readily to the tongue as saying *Cattleya warscewiczii!*

There are more laelias than there are cattleyas, and the genus *Laelia* by our count here numbers 59 species, one a natural hybrid population. Two species include varietas populations. Our Brazilian friends have intimated that there are at least two or three more as yet undescribed rock laelias to come. So, there are a few more species of *Laelia* than *Cattleya.* Also, I am told that the Mexican orchidologists will divide certain species into new ones so that the total will rise still further. As ecology, pollination, lip configurations and distribution patterns are better understood, this splitting becomes an inevitable outcome. For the hobbyist it may mean a new label on an old plant and confusion about current names and parentages. But to the botanist-taxonomist it indicates a clearer understanding of the speciation processes that have taken place in nature over eons of time and count-less generations of plants. Once again I'm impressed by what seems to be a frozen moment in time—catching the evolutionary processes of the orchid family in active transition, brought to a sudden stop by our current viewing, like a single frame of an on-going movie.

This volume follows the same format as Volume I. One of the first ele-ments is the hybrid list in Table I, followed by tables with the classification outlines used by earlier and more recent investigators. As with the cattleyas, I have found that none of the systems is totally consistent with observations of flower and plant detail, nor with the International Rules of Botanical Nomenclature. I have, accordingly, presented my own revisions and a system that I hope is in accordance with the Rules, resolving some of the nomenclatural confusions that have existed in the literature for many years.

But the reader, expecting a steady-state for labeling and parentage, should not forget that taxonomy and classification, like the orchids them-selves, are dynamic subjects always open to better understanding and to revisions. For example, having closed the research and writing for Volume I, so it could be published, I have since learned that *Cattleya silvana* is a bona fide species and should no longer be considered "questionable", as it was styled in that volume. It deserves a description with illustration, and indeed will be so treated in a later *Emendatio*, as will other species that may emerge from present obscurity. Such species haven't all been found, nor have they all been described, even in popular and important genera such as *Cattleya* or *Laelia*. Also, as another example, five more hybrid genera should be added to the list of intergeneric epithets in Volume I: *Westara, Kraussara, Mailamaiara, Fialaara* and *Johnyeeara,* the last the first sexta-generic hybrid in the *Cattleya* Alliance.

We are currently aware of a certain urgency in doing critical field work and preserving herbarium as well as living plant material—perhaps with no more than 10–20 years to spare. Otherwise, the destruction of natural habitats may eliminate certain species before they are ever seen the first time! Many species totter on the edge of obliteration, yet the Endangered Species Convention, to which many nations now belong, does little to stop deforestation and local destruction but does add to our ever-present bureaucratic procedures and officiousness. The problems are com-plicated ones and have no simple solutions, but we must keep in mind that "Extinction is Forever"!

Vuilleumier has recently made the point that biomes with great species density should have the greatest number of conservation areas set aside. In Latin America, where the cattleyas and their relatives reside in their respective biomes, many such areas are critical, particularly the Andean cloud forests and the lowland Colombian and Ecuadorian forests. In fact, the whole of Ecuador, a country the size of the state of Colorado, with at least 10 percent of the world's orchids, *should* be a major conserva-tion area But it's already too late—not because of collectors, I would emphasize, but because of local destruction of forests and habitats for dwellings and agriculture.

I emphasize these points because so many orchids have only a localized distribution and thus a whole species population could be wiped out with the destruction of a fairly limited area—one mountain ridge, one ravine, one valley—burned up in a single fire! We have learned that the orchid family has been in a rapid, indeed almost explosive, to use one author's terminology, state of evolution. This means that many species have not had a chance to spread widely, particularly if natural barriers such as water, mountains, wide plains, or differences in altitude or habitat are involved. As I explained in the first volume, geography is often for me a deciding factor in describing separate species. In some cases, as with the rock laelias in this volume, the location becomes a crucial criterion. This closely related group is widespread in central Brazil, yet differentiated in localized areas according to rock substrate, altitude of habitat, habit of growth, flowering season or flower color, into its component taxa. The classification presented in this book is certainly not the last word, and we should keep an open mind about ways to improve the subdivisions to reflect better the processes that have gone on in nature. In trying to devise a key for the *Parviflorae* one becomes all too aware of how arbitrarily some of the species are separated. And if your plant doesn't match mine closely, we can both be in difficulty.

One of the unique things about the laelias is their distribution in Brazil, Central America and México. Unlike the cattleyas, there are no *Laelia* species in Andean regions of South America nor in the northern portions of South America that can connect the two areas. Perhaps eventually we'll have an explanation of how the disjunction came about.

The question of "how to grow" is important to many readers, and yet the requirements of the laelias are so similar, in general, to those of the cattleyas, that a separate horticultural treatment seems unnecessary in this volume. Whenever habitat niches dictate that a different cultural treatment is needed, it will be described under the appropriate species involved. This volume closes with an itemizing of "questionable species" followed by a bibliographic list for more detailed reading on a given species or a given group or area.

Once again I must express my appreciation and thanks to the many people who have wished me well with this project and have helped it along. An accolade goes to Dr. Leslie Garay, who has lent his expertise on technical details and on matters of *Laelia* taxonomy and Latin usage. I also single out for mention Marie Long, Research Librarian at the New York Botanical Garden, who found many of my missing references and type descriptions; Evelyn Darrow, Inter-library Loans, at Western Washington University where I am a Biology Dept. Research Associate; Trudi Marsh, who took so many fine photographs and lent them for use in the book; Red Marsh, who grew many of the plants so that they could be flowered and photographed by his wife; Dr. Jack Fowlie, who helped with both photos and his many publications based on sometimes difficult fieldwork and firsthand observations along with Denis Duveen; Jorge Verboonen and his son, Mauricio, present owners and operators of Orquidário Binot in Petrópolis, Brazil, who have given much good advice based on years of experience and handling thousands of plants, also some of the photos; Hugh Henry, whose fine photos (including the jacket cover for the cattleya volume) are invaluable; Mary Noble McQuerry, who helped me obtain some of the prints reproduced in these volumes; and, finally, my wife, Pat, who continues to straighten out my grammar, has an eagle eye for proof errors and absolutely dotes on finding apostrophes out of place. The staff at Timber Press has been most supportive and understanding, and I still admire their editor, Richard Abel, despite all the corrections he makes on my manuscripts. He always says, "Let's tighten it up! It's just a suggestion—you don't have to use it." But, I usually do. With such encouraging help at this time, I now look forward to the work on Volume III. I've always liked jigsaw puzzles, and this book has been a fine one to assemble!

Photo credits are acknowledged in the picture captions. As in Volume I, those pictures without credits have been taken by the author.

June 19, 1989

CHAPTER 1

The Genus *Laelia* and Its Classification

Before this genus was formally established by Lindley in 1831, many of the species started out with the name of *Cattleya*. Others have been called *Bletia* at one time or another. Reading all the synonyms of the species, one realizes that there has been a great variety of opinions regarding *Laelia* classification—both with respect to what a species might be called as well as what the genus actually includes. In the final analysis it comes down to the number of pollinia in the flower—eight, contrasting with the four pollinia of *Cattleya*—plus characteristics the plants *don't* have that are present in other genera with the same number of pollinia.

The genus *Laelia* was founded on the species *Laelia grandiflora*, from México. This species had previously been named *Bletia grandiflora* by La Llave and Lexarza in 1825, and before that *Bletia speciosa* by Humboldt, Bonpland and Kunth in 1815. Its proper name, by modern rulings, must therefore be *Laelia speciosa*, which also invalidates Lindley's later 1839 name for this species, *Laelia majalis*. In his genus description Lindley does not mention why he chose *Laelia* for these plants, but we know that Laelia was one of the Vestal Virgins. It was also the name borne by the females of the patrician Roman family of Laelius. Having *Laelia* species in orchid collections was considerably more popular in the past than it is at present, but their bright colors and ease of cultivation still give them a place with the connoisseur. The intergeneric hybrid list (Table I) shows they are far from being neglected.

Only two of our present *Laelia* species were included in the genus when it was first established, *L. speciosa* (as *Laelia grandiflora*) and *L. autumnalis*. *Cattleya* (now *Laeliopsis*) *domingensis* was also included as a likely member of the group, but its number of pollinia and foliage were not then known. Lindley said in describing the new genus that it was near to *Cattleya*, but had eight pollinia, leathery leaves "sitting" on the pseudobulbs and a labellum facing outwards from the axis of the flower. These basic characteristics are not terribly definitive, so it is not surprising that a variety of species has been placed within *Laelia* and then later removed to form other genera, particularly plants we now call *Schomburgkia*.

In 1842 Lindley proposed the first classification of the laelias, separating them into two groups: the *Grandiflorae* with petals larger than the sepals, and the *Parviflorae* with the same sized sepals and petals. As various botanists described new species in the genus, these groups were modified until Pfitzer published his synopsis with five sections in 1889. Schlechter in 1917 proposed the system that is, basically, still the system in use today. Schlechter's key to the sections, translated from the original German, plus the other systems with their included species, may be found in Table II.

Laelia is as varied a group as *Cattleya*, which contains some of its nearest relatives, but the former's geographic distribution is not so diverse even though the genus contains more species. In contrast to *Cattleya*, *Laelia* is found only in Brazil, México and some of Central America. There are no Andean species, nor any in the northern portions of South America, nor in the Caribbean. *Laelia* has, nevertheless, about 59 species to the 52 of *Cattleya*.

Opinions based on the geography of the species, as well as flower and plant characteristics, have held that the Méxican and Central American species, as well as the rock laelias in Brazil, each belong in separate genera. This means the balance of the species would require a third, or even more generic names since *Laelia* would remain attached to the Méxican-Central American group containing *Laelia speciosa*, the type species for the genus. Such a further splitting of the present genus would not give us a better understanding of how the subgroups originated, and, it seems to me, the equivalent is achieved by the subgeneric categories in the various classification schemes. A division into three or more new genera would in addition create horticultural confusion with all the necessary name changes. It just doesn't seem sensible to have a "splitter's" approach to this particular classification problem.

The genus *Hoffmannseggella* was published for the rock laelia taxon by H. G. Jones in 1968, and he included those species that fall in the subgenus *Cyrtolaelia* of Schlechter's 1917 classification system (the *Parviflorae* of Lindley). The new genus was based on *L. cinnabarina*, and there is little question but that the many rock laelia species within this group are a natural taxon with related habitat niches, geographical distribution, flower pigmentation and flower configuration. Nevertheless, *Hoffmannseggella* has not been used to date, any more than the limiting of the genus *Laelia* to only the Méxican and Central American species. Should the genus ever be split into its various parts as new genera, then *Hoffmannseggella* would come into its own as a valid generic name.

Hoffmannsegg in 1843 actually intended to name the rock laelias as members of a new genus, *Amalias*, but he did not validly publish the name, and it was never used. Jones has now dealt with those original intentions but has named the genus after Hoffmannsegg himself, rather than publishing *Amalias* as a valid entity.

At present there is no available older name for the balance of the Brazilian laelias, with the exception of *Bletia* mentioned above, and that is no longer a valid nor accurate choice. If the laelias were to be subdivided into three major groups, the logical choice for the Brazilian species, excluding the rock laelias, would be *Cattleyodes*. This was proposed by Schlechter in 1917 (Table II) as a sectional name and could be raised to the genus level to accommodate these Brazilian species. By the same process his *Microlaelia* for *L. lundii*, and his *Hadrolaelia* could become genera, and then we would only have to find new generic names for *L. perrinii* with its unique column structure and flower configuration, for *L. sincorana* with its mixture of *Hadrolaelia*-like flowers and rupicolous vegetative habits, and possibly for *L. virens* with its small, cleistogamous flowers.

Since eight pollinia represent a primitive evolutionary state of orchid development, the laelias may be thought of as closer to their ancestral line than the cattleyas with their four pollinia. This would indicate that the cattleyas are a more derived group from their ancestors than the laelias; have undergone a greater degree of change as they spread and evolved to present day species; have reduced their pollinia from eight to four. The diversity of the laelias also shows overlap of flower form with the labiate cattleyas, and the vegetative habits overlap with both *Encyclia* and *Schomburgkia* (see Withner and Adams, 1960). Brazilian species, with the exception of *L. lundii*, are unifoliate on mature growths. The Méxican-Central American species are, by contrast, mostly two or three-leaved. All things considered, the qualities and characteristics of *Laelia* give it a "central" position, along with *Schomburgkia*, in the evolution of the Laeliinae. Their geographic distribution also fits that position central to the other genera.

In addition to the Schlechter system mentioned above, and the earlier one of Pfitzer, there are also the systems of Pabst and Dungs and of Brieger, Maatsch and Senghas, but there is no Latin nor typification accompanying their terminology to provide valid publication, according to the Rules, of the epithets. For the system used in this book (Tables III and IV) the various subgenera and sections are briefly summarized (also see Table VII). These descriptions consist of so-called "key" characters, qualities that are diagnostic for each group. The Subgenus *Laelia* consists of plants of Méxican or Central American origin, in contrast to the Subgenus *Crispae* with species that are only found in Brazil. The Subgenus *Parviflorae*, with only the rock laelias, is also Brazilian, as is *Microlaelia* with its single species.

The Méxican-Central American taxa are distinctly pseudobulbous in the fashion of encyclias, having mostly pear-shaped, ridged or furrowed, angled or flattened, shapes. Except for *L. speciosa*, in the section *Laelia*, with its comparatively short flower stems without nodes or sheaths, and its one or two flowers, most species have elongated flower stalks with several nodes and sheaths and several flowers concentrated at the tips of the racemes. These latter species constitute the section *Podolaelia*. Their flowering habit plus the two or three leaves, the presence of definite keels or ridges on the clearly three-lobed lips, and the photophilic habits of the plants, may be called schomburgkia-like qualities. Mrs. Adams and I characterized these various groups in our 1960 paper at the World Orchid Conference in London.

Schlechter—who first used the term *Podolaelia*, the footed laelias, in 1917—does not tell us why he called them footed—whether it was in reference to some detail of the flower or some detail of the growth habit of the plants. Most likely it was in reference to the somewhat footed or stalked pseudobulbs present in *L. anceps*, but this is not stated as such. With the exception of *L. rubescens* which extends in distribution into Costa Rica and Panama, these laelias are found only in the Méxican *tierra fria*.

The Subgenus *Crispae*, an epithet based on Pfitzer's 1889 system, consists only of Brazilian species. Brieger and his colleagues used *Brasilienses* in the third edition of *Schlechter's Die Orchideen* for the same group, but the name was never validly published. For this book, therefore, the name *Crispae* must be used, even though it does not immediately tell the reader about the origins of the species involved. This subgenus includes three sections.

The *Crispae* are definitely cattleya-like. They have large monofoliate photophilic plants, prominent sheaths for the flower buds, flowers with poorly defined or no lateral lobes set off in the lips, and no keels or ridges on the midlobes. The later name of Schlechter, *Cattleyodes*, emphasized these points.

The term *Hadrolaelia*, a Schlechter designation without explanation, means "thick" laelia, but we don't know why—thick leaves or what? It could be the thickened or keeled veins of the lip, but likely it refers to the "thickened stems", sometimes hardly pseudobulbous, found on plants that have grown in low light. These laelias are generally like miniature cattleyas in their overall habit of growth, perhaps more distinctly pseudobulbous in high-light forms, but they lack a flower sheath, and the young leaf substitutes for it by folding around the developing flowers. The lateral lobes are somewhat delineated but with no distinct sinuses to set them off. These hadrolaelias all have definite keels or ridges on the midlobes of the lips and in general appear closest to *L. speciosa* from México, the type species for the genus.

The debate—begun in the 1890s, with opinions from Veitch, Schlechter, Rolfe, the International Orchid Commission, and others—still continues over the status of *L. pumila* vs. *L. praestans* in the *Hadrolaelia*. To complicate matters further, my research reveals that the proper name for *L. praestans* is *L. spectabilis*. They, *pumila* and *spectabilis*, are being treated as separate species in this book as each population seems to have distinct qualities. The fact that the two species have possibly hybridized in nature, making a difficult complex where characteristics overlap, does not make the job easier.

In my estimation, some of the clones of awarded *L. pumila* that we can read about in the American Orchid Society *Awards Quarterly* or *Bulletin* are in reality *L. spectabilis* (*praestans*). That species naturally possesses more of the qualities judges look for in orchid flowers than do the flowers of *L. pumila*, and few orchidists manage to make the distinction between the two. Should anyone be interested in pursuing the matter further, I would suggest the flowers be checked on their next blooming. As far as I can observe from the award photographs, both species are labeled *pumila*, yet some flowers are unquestionably *spectabilis*.

Another species, ordinarily placed with the hadrolaelias, also causes some problems for me. The lips of the flowers of *L. sincorana* do show distinct lobing. In fact, *L. sincorana* is so distinctive in its lobed lip structure and its short, stubby, thickened and pseudobulbous growth, that one may make a case here for putting it in its own section and not lumping it with the other species in *Hadrolaelia*. It provides a transition between the *Crispae* subgenus and the rock species of the *Parviflorae* complex. Placing it in its own section, *Sincoranae*, with only the single species, resolves the difficulties.

The section *Perriniae*, also with its single species, *L. perrinii*, is distinguished by the unique shape of the column and the configuration of the flower. It is, otherwise, more like a member of the *Crispae*. If we knew more about its natural pollinators compared to the other species perhaps these structural features could be better explained.

Subgenus *Microlaelia* also has only one species, *L. lundii*, a miniature plant with a creeping habit of growth. It has distinct, fusiform pseudobulbs, and they are bifoliate with nearly terete leaves. It is not like any other laelia, and even Schlechter commented upon its unique qualities in the genus. But he didn't go so far as to consider placing it in a genus all its own, though that has certainly been suggested from time to time. The subgenus rank still seems appropriate.

The complex of species, now numbering at least 35, that are generally called the rock, or rupicolous, laelias are in the subgenus *Parviflorae*. They are still a most confusing group to us as so little is known about some of them, and they have only been described in the last few years. One of my friends in Brazil calls them the "ru-pickles", perhaps with good reason. For some of the species we barely have more than the original Latin description and perhaps a line drawing. They are poorly known in cultivation, and obtaining photos or other information is often difficult. The publications in the *Orchid Digest* have been most useful, amplifying the Latin type descriptions and, in fact, have provided most of the information in English up to the present time on these species. Dr. Fowlie's information, as a result of his many study trips to Brazil and his position as editor of that publication, cannot be equaled, and I most gratefully acknowledge his efforts, without which the accounts of the species in this section would have been comparatively meager. Everyone should have had the *Orchid Digest* reprint of the papers by Guido Pabst, Denis Duveen and Jack Fowlie on the section *Parviflorae*. Pabst was the major Brazilian botanist interested in the group, so that many of the species bear his authorship. Duveen is an ardent collector, grower and writer on Brazilian species, a "jungle-basher" in his own words.

These taxa were collectively called *Cyrtolaelia* by Schlechter, the name meaning curved or reflexed, referring to the way the apex of the lip was curled back and under the rest of the lip. But Lindley's earlier term, *Parviflorae*, distinguishing them from the larger-flowered *Crispae* type of laelia, has the priority for a subgeneric epithet. They are a distinct group, and with three exceptions are rock inhabiting with a distinctive type of habit. The plants are usually monofoliate; have a flower sheath; have cylindrically shaped pseudobulbs sometimes with basal enlargement; and are often flushed with red color on either the whole plant or just the reverse of the leaves as a result of their exposure to the direct sunlight. As noted earlier, they were intended to be placed in a separate genus, *Amalias*, by Hoffmannsegg, and *Hoffmannseggella* by Jones; but neither of these concepts has been accepted by present-day orchidologists.

The subdivision of the *Parviflorae* is still "in progress", and no definitive system can truly be offered until more is known about all of the species. The systems so far seem arbitrary and artificial but point the way at least. Seven character states have been emphasized: epiphytic vs. actual rupicolous habitat niche; flower color; whether or not the midlobe of the lip is provided with a distinct isthmus or is sessile; relative size of flower parts; length of the flower stalk in comparison to the height of the leaf; season of bloom; and habitat location.

The flower colors are either orange or red-orange, yellow, or various forms of purple, lavender or rose. These classes of colors are also distinctive among the cattleyas, the yellow group having carotenoid pigmentations, the purple group being predominantly anthocyanin colors, and the reds and oranges a combination of the two systems. The flower stalk height seems somewhat relative as a key character in classification, but some of these species have short stalks with the flowers held at about leaf height, and others have elongated stalks with the flowers held as much as two or three times the height of the leaves. Even with these main characteristics as a guide, the group continues to be confusing; descriptions in various books do not always jibe and some of the species within the groups are difficult to distinguish clearly. Only a few have qualities that make them unmistakable. Pabst's key, updated by Fowlie and Duveen, has provided the best information to date, and now Table V presents a new key with my approach to the problems presented by these 35 species. Since the whole group is comparatively new in cultivation, most species having been found only in the last 25 years, neither the names nor the appearances are yet "automatic" for either the judges or the hobby grower. As further aids, lip outlines are presented in Figure 2, and a listing of relative lip sizes is given in Table VI with field marks in Table VII.

The terms *Cinnabarinae, Flavae* and *Lilacinae* have been used by Ghillány to describe sections of this subgenus *Parviflorae,* but so far as I can find these epithets have not been formally published for such usage. Pabst and Dungs use the alliance approach without giving the alliances sectional epithets. Brieger, Maatsch and Senghas (Table II) provide six subgroups, each named after the lead species in the subgroup. However, several of the current species are not included in their survey, nor are they mentioned as synonyms, so we are still left up in the air with their work on the matter of rupicolous laelias. In the system presented here five sections are used, each named after the oldest or the most representative species in the taxon, but this is not to say that a better system is not possible.

The Section *Harpophyllae* has epiphytic species, flower stalks shorter than the leaf, flowers orange or yellow, and the pseudobulbs are unthickened, thin and pencil-like. The rest of the sections are rock inhabiting, sometimes on very specific sorts of rock: hematite, sandstone, *pedra cange,* gneiss or granite.

The Section *Parviflorae,* with flower stalks much higher than the leaf (2–4 times) has red, orange or yellow flowers. The base of the pseudobulbs can be distinctly thickened in diameter and they are mostly elongated. This section includes species with the largest flowers and plants in the subgenus, yet they are called *Parviflorae* by the Rules.

The Section *Esalqueanae* consists of miniature rock-inhabiting plants with yellow flowers. The flower stalks are only the height of the leaves, sometimes a little higher.

The Section *Rupestres* includes the larger rupicolous species with lilac or rose-purple flowers. They have elongated flower stalks, usually 2–4 times higher than the leaves.

The Section *Liliputanae* has tiny inhabitants of rock crevices with their flower stalks as high or only a little higher than the leaves. The flowers are lilac or purple-pink, but three species have contrasting yellow lips instead of the flower parts being all the same color.

TABLE I

**Intergeneric Combinations with *Laelia*
Registered through May, 1990,
With Approved Abbreviations**

LAELIA

× *Barkeria*	= *Laeliokeria (Lkra.)*
× *Barkeria* × *Cattleya*	= *Laeliocatkeria (Lcka.)*
× *Barkeria* × *Sophronitis*	= *Staalara (Staal.)*
× *Brassavola*	= *Brassolaelia (Bl.)*
× *Brassavola* × *Broughtonia* × *Cattleya*	= *Otaara (Otr.)*
× *Brassavola* × *Broughtonia* × *Cattleya* × *Epidendrum*	= *Hattoriara (Hatt.)*
× *Brassavola* × *Broughtonia* × *Cattleya* × *Schomburgkia*	= *Westara (Wsta.)*
× *Brassavola* × *Broughtonia* × *Cattleya* × *Sophronitis*	= *Hasegawaara (Hasgw.)*
× *Brassavola* × *Cattleya*	= *Brassolaeliocattleya (Blc.)*
× *Brassavola* × *Cattleya* × *Diacrium*	= *Iwanagara (Iwan.)*
× *Brassavola* × *Cattleya* × *Domingoa* × *Epidendrum*	= *Kawamotoara (Kwmta.)*
× *Brassavola* × *Cattleya* × *Epidendrum*	= *Yamadara (Yam.)*
× *Brassavola* × *Cattleya* × *Epidendrum* × *Schomburgkia*	= *Yahiroara (Yhra.)*
× *Brassavola* × *Cattleya* × *Epidendrum* × *Schomburgkia* × *Sophronitis*	= *Johnyeeara (Jya.)*
× *Brassavola* × *Cattleya* × *Epidendrum* × *Sophronitis*	= *Rothara (Roth.)*
× *Brassavola* × *Cattleya* × *Schomburgkia*	= *Recchara (Recc.)*
× *Brassavola* × *Cattleya* × *Schomburgkia* × *Sophronitis*	= *Fergusonara (Ferg.)*
× *Brassavola* × *Cattleya* × *Sophronitis*	= *Potinara (Pot.)*
× *Brassavola* × *Epidendrum*	= *Brassoepilaelia (Bpl.)*
× *Brassavola* × *Schomburgkia*	= *Maclemoreara (Mclmra.)*
× *Brassavola* × *Sophronitis*	= *Lowara (Low.)*
× *Broughtonia*	= *Laelonia (Lna.)*
× *Broughtonia* × *Cattleya*	= *Laeliocatonia (Lctna.)*
× *Broughtonia* × *Cattleya* × *Epidendrum*	= *Jewellara (Jwa.)*

× *Broughtonia* × *Cattleya* × *Epidendrum* × *Sophronitis* = *Buiara (Bui.)*

× *Broughtonia* × *Cattleya* × *Laeliopsis* = *Fialaara (Fia.)*

× *Broughtonia* × *Cattleya* × *Sophronitis* = *Hawkinsara (Hknsa.)*

× *Broughtonia* × *Laeliopsis* = *Jimenezara (Jmzra.)*

× *Broughtonia* × *Sophronitis* = *Hartara (Hart.)*

× *Cattleya* = *Laeliocattleya (Lc.)*

× *Cattleya* × *Diacrium* = *Dialaeliocattleya (Dialc.)*

× *Cattleya* × *Diacrium* × *Epidendrum* = *Allenara (Alna.)*

× *Cattleya* × *Diacrium* × *Schomburgkia* = *Mailamaiara (Mai.)*

× *Cattleya* × *Diacrium* × *Sophronitis* = *Higashiara (Hgsh.)*

× *Cattleya* × *Epidendrum* = *Epilaeliocattleya (Eplc.)*

× *Cattleya* × *Epidendrum* × *Schomburgkia* = *Northenara (Nrna.)*

× *Cattleya* × *Epidendrum* × *Schomburgkia* × *Sophronitis* = *Izumiara (Izma.)*

× *Cattleya* × *Epidendrum* × *Sophronitis* = *Kirchara (Kir.)*

× *Cattleya* × *Schomburgkia* = *Lyonara (Lyon.)*

× *Cattleya* × *Schomburgkia* × *Sophronitis* = *Herbertara (Hbtr.)*

× *Cattleya* × *Sophronitis* = *Sophrolaeliocattleya (Slc.)*

× *Diacrium* = *Dialaelia (Dial.)*

× *Diacrium* × *Schomburgkia* = *Klehmara (Klma.)*

× *Diacrium* × *Sophronitis* = *Severinara (Sev.)*

× *Epidendrum* = *Epilaelia (Epl.)*

× *Epidendrum* × *Schomburgkia* = *Dillonara (Dill.)*

× *Epidendrum* × *Sophronitis* = *Stanfieldara (Sfdra.)*

× *Laeliopsis* = *Liaopsis (Liaps.)*

× *Leptotes* = *Leptolaelia (Lptl.)*

× *Schomburgkia* = *Schombolaelia (Smbl.)*

× *Schomburgkia* × *Sophronitis* = *Deiselara (Dsla.)*

× *Sophronitis* = *Sophrolaelia (Sl.)*

TABLE II

**Outline of *Laelia* classification schemes
of previous authors**

Lindley's classification in *Botanical Register,*
1842, 28:sub t. 62.

Section 1. *Grandiflorae*—petals larger than sepals—*autum-nalis, majalis, anceps, superbiens, perrinii, rubescens, albida.*

Section 2. *Parviflorae*—petals same size as sepals—*flava, cinnabarina, rupestris.*

Pfitzer's classification in *Die Naturlichen Pflanzenfamilien,* 1889,
p. 147–148.

Section I. *Crispae.* Labiate flowers like those of *C. mossiae.* Lip scarcely 3-lobed, smooth—*crispa, purpurata*

Section II. *Violaceae.* Pseudobulbs egg-shaped, lip poorly 3-lobed, smooth—*peduncularis*

Section III. *Speciosae.* Pseudobulbs egg-shaped. Lip clearly 3-lobed—*autumnalis, furfuracea*

Section IV. *Lancibracteae.* With long bracts below the flowers—*superbiens*

Section V. *Digbyana.* Habit of *Crispae,* but tube of lip shorter. Plant gray-green—*digbyana*

Cogniaux's classification of the genus *Laelia* in
Martius' Flora Brasiliensis, 1901 (1898–1902).

Subgenus I. *Eulaelia*
Section *Monophyllae*
1. *Crispatae*—lips deeply 3-lobed *crispa, cinnamomea, cinnabarina, crispilabia, longipes, rupestris, flava, caulescens, harpophylla*
2. *Lobatae*—lips scarcely 3-lobed *xanthina, lobata, jongheana, pumila, grandis, purpurata, perrinii*
Section *Diphyllae*—*lindleyana, cattleyoides, regnellii, lundii*
Subgenus II. *Laelio-cattleya*—*elegans, amanda, porphyritis*

Schlechter's 1917 Classification of the genus *Laelia;*
a key to the sections. In *Orchis,* 1917, 11(5):87–96.

A. Lip without keels or ridges internally—*Cattleyodes: crispa, grandis, grandis* var. *tenebrosa, Johniana, lobata, Perrinii, purpurata, xanthina*

AA. Lip with internal crests or keels
  a. Floral stem without nodes and without sheaths
    I. Petals clearly larger than the sepals
      1. Pseudobulbs consisting of a single internode—*Hadrolaelia: Jongheana, pumila, pumila* var. *Dayana, pumila* var. *praestans*
      2. Pseudobulbs of more than one internode—*Eulaelia: speciosa*
    II. Petals and sepals more or less equal in size—*Microlaelia: cattleyoides, Lundii, Regnelli*
  aa. Floral stalk with nodes and sheaths
    I. Sepals and petals little different; floral stalks with a

large sheath—*Cyrtolaelia: caulescens,
cinnabarina, crispilabia, flava, harpophylla,
longipes, longipes* var. *Lucasiana, rupestris*
II. Petals much larger than the sepals; floral stalks
without sheaths
1. Pseudobulbs with two leaves; lip with keels,
not teeth—*Podolaelia: albida, anceps,
autumnalis, furfuracea, Gouldiana, peduncularis, rubescens*
2. Pseudobulbs with two leaves; lip with
prominent crests and teeth—*Calolaelia:
superbiens*

Brazilian laelias according to Pabst and Dungs
in *Orchidaceae Brasilienses,* vol. 1, 1975.

Laelia
Section *Cattleyodes*—plants similar to the unifoliate
cattleyas
*crispa, fidelensis grandis, lobata, perrinii, pur-
purata, tenebrosa, virens, xanthina*
Section *Hadrolaelia*—inflorescence without a sheath; lip
with keels
*alaorii, dayana, jongheana, praestans, pumila,
sincorana*
Section *Microlaelia*—plants small, bifoliate with almost
fusiform pseudobulbs and terete leaves.
cattleyodes, lundii
Section *Parviflorae*—plants usually rupicolous (except for
harpophylla Alliance), pseudobulbs obclavate
Laelia harpophylla Alliance—plants epiphytic,
inflorescence shorter than leaf
brevicaulis, harpophylla, kautskyi
Laelia crispata Alliance—flowers lilac or purplish,
inflorescence much higher than leaf
*caulescens, crispata, crispilabia, mantiqueirae,
longipes, pfisteri*
Laelia liliputana Alliance—as above, but inflorescence
only a little higher than leaf
ghillanyi, liliputana, lucasiana, milletii, reginae
Laelia flava Alliance—flowers yellow, orange or red;
inflorescence much higher than the leaf
*angereri, bahiensis, blumenscheinii, briegeri,
cinnabarina, cinnamomea, endsfeldzii, flava,
gloedeniana, macrobulbosa, milleri, mixta*
Laelia esalqueana Alliance—as above, but inflorescence only a little higher than leaf
bradei, esalqueana, itambana

Classification of *Laelia* according to Brieger, Maatsch and
Senghas in *Schlechter's Die Orchideen* (3rd edition), 1981.

I. Subgenus *(Eu)Laelia*
Section 1. *(Eu)Laelia*—*speciosa*
Section 2. *Podolaelia*—*furfuracea, autumnalis, gouldiana,
anceps, albida, rubescens*
II. Subgenus *Brasilienses*
Section 3. *Crispae*—*purpurata, crispa, lobata, grandis,
tenebrosa, fidelensis, xanthina, virens*

Section 4. *Perrinii—perrinii*
Section 5. *Microlaelia—lundii*
Section 6. *Parviflorae*
    Subsection 1. *Harpophyllae—harpophylla, kautskyi*
    Subsection 2. *Lucasianae—lucasiana,*
        esalqueana
    Subsection 3. *Caulescentes—longipes, ghillanyi,*
        caulescens, rupestris, tereticaulis, pfisteri
    Subsection 4. *Bahiensis—bahiensis, briegeri, itambana*
    Subsection 5. *Flavae—flava, milleri, mixta, gloedeniana*
    Subsection 6. *Cinnabarinae—cinnabarina, cowanii*
Section 7. *Hadrolaelia—jongheana, oliverii, pumila* subsp.
    pumila, pumila subsp. *dayana, pumila* subsp. *praestans,*
    sincorana

TABLE III

Laelia classification scheme used in this book

Genus *Laelia*

Subgenus *Laelia*—plants native to México or Central America
    Section *Laelia*—flower stalks without nodes or sheaths
        speciosa
    Section *Podolaelia*—flower stalks elongated, with nodes and sheaths
        albida, anceps, autumnalis, bancalarii, furfuracea, gouldiana, rubescens, (rubescens var. *aurea)*
Subgenus *Crispae*—plants native to Brazil
    Section *Crispae*—plants unifoliate, similar to the monofoliate cattleyas
        crispa, elegans, fidelensis, grandis, lobata, purpurata, tenebrosa, virens, xanthina
    Section *Perriniae*—flower with column coming to a narrowing and tapered tip
        perrinii
    Section *Hadrolaelia*—inflorescence without a sheath, but young leaf folding around buds; the lip with keels, unlobed; leaves leathery
        alaorii, dayana, jongheana, spectabilis, pumila
    Section *Sincoranae*—lip keeled and with lateral lobes; leaves thick, succulent, channeled, and rigid
        sincorana
Subgenus *Microlaelia*—plants small, bifoliate, with fusiform pseudobulbs; creeping habit of growth; no sheath, 5 keels on lip; plants Brazilian
    lundii
Subgenus *Parviflorae*—plants Brazilian; unifoliate, mostly growing on rock; flowers comparatively small, stalk developing from a sheath; midlobe curving back and under
    Section *Harpophyllae*—plants epiphytic; stems un-thickened, pencil-like; flower stalk shorter than leaf; flowers orange or yellow
        brevicaulis, harpophylla, kautskyana
    Section *Parviflorae*—plants rupicolous; flower stalk much higher than leaf, 2–4 times; flowers red, orange or yellow
        angereri, bahiensis, blumenscheinii, briegeri, cardimii, cinnabarina, endsfeldzii, flava, gloedeniana, gracilis, milleri, mixta, sanguiloba
    Section *Esalqueanae*—plants rupicolous; flower stalk only as high or a little higher than leaf; flowers yellow
        bradei, esalqueana, itambana
    Section *Rupestres*—plants rupicolous; flower stalk much higher than leaf, 2–4 times, flowers lilac or purple
        caulescens, crispata, crispilabia, gardneri, hispidula, mantiqueirae, pfisteri, tereticaulis
    Section *Liliputanae*—plants rupicolous; flower stalk slightly higher than leaf; flowers lilac or purplish
        duveenii, ghillanyi, kettieana, liliputana, longipes, lucasiana, reginae

18   *The Cattleyas* II

TABLE IV

**Latin diagnoses for the *Laelia* classification system
presented in this book**

Subgenus *Laelia* Lindley. Type: *L. speciosa* (H. B. and K.) Schlecter.
  Section *Laelia* Lindley. Type: *L. speciosa* (H. B. and K.) Schlechter. *Scapus sine nodis vel bracteis.*
  Section *Podolaelia* Schlechter. Lectotype: *L. anceps* Lindley. *Scapus elongatus cum nodis et bracteis.*
Subgenus *Crispae* (Pfitz.) Withner *c. nov.* Basionym:
  Section *Crispae* Pfitzer. Type: *L. crispa* Rchb. f. *Plantae brasilienses; petalis quam sepalis multo latioribus.*
  Section *Crispae* Pfitzer. Lectotype: *L. crispa* Rchb. f. *Plantae unifoliatae; grandiflorae; labello aliquantulum trilobato; columna non sigmoidea.*
  Section *Perriniae* Withner. Type: *L. perrinii* Lindley. *Plantae unifoliatae, grandiflorae; labello aliquantulum trilobato; columna elongata, antice satis concava, sigmoidea, apicem versus angustiora.*
  Section *Hadrolaelia* Schlechter. Lectotype: *L. pumila.* (Hooker) Rchb. f. *Plantae unifoliatae; foliis juvenilibus facientes spathae; labello aliquantum lobato, 3–5 carinato.*
  Section *Sinocoranae* Withner. Type: *L. sincorana* Schlechter. *Plantae unifoliatae; foliis crassis, canaliculatis, rigidentibus; labello trilobato.*
Subgenus *Microlaelia* (Schlechter) Withner *c. nov.* Basionym:
  Section *Microlaelia* Schlechter. Lectotype: *L. lundii* Rchb. f. *Pseudobulbis bifoliatis; foliis semicylindraceis, linearibus; rhizomate repenti, elongato; spatha deficienti; labello trilobato, 5-costato.*
Subgenus *Parviflorae* (Lindley) Withner *c. nov.* Basionym:
  Section *Parviflorae* Lindley. Lectotype: *L. flava* Lindley. *Plantae brasilienses; sepalis petalisque inter se simillibus.*
  Section *Harpophyllae* Withner. Type: *L. harpophylla* Rchb. f. *Plantae epiphyticae; pseudobulbis unifoliatis, satis gracilibus, teretiusculis; foliis elongatis, anguste ligulatis.*
  Section *Parviflorae* Lindley. Lectotype: *L. flava* Lindley. *Plantae rupicolae; scapo folio multo longiori; floribus rubris, aurantiacis vel flavis.*
  Section *Esalqueanae* Withner. Type: *L. esalqueana* Blumenschein. *Plantae rupicolae; scapo folio plus minusve aequali vel paulo breviori; floribus flavis.*
  Section *Rupestres* Withner. Type: *L. crispata* (Thunb.) Garay. *Plantae rupicolae; scapo folio multo longiori; floribus lilacinis vel purpureis.*
  Section *Liliputanae* Withner. Type: *L. liliputana* Pabst. *Plantae rupicolae, diminuativae; scapo folio plus minusve aequali vel paulo breviori; floribus lilacinis vel purpureis.*

TABLE V

Numbered Key to Species of Subgenus *Parviflorae* of the Genus *Laelia*

(Lip shapes are described and measurements are made when the lip or other flower parts are spread out and flattened as much as possible. See lip outlines in Fig. 2. Cultural conditions will affect size measurements, *i.e.* stalk length, pseudobulb height or shape, etc.)

1. Stems not thickened, pencil-like, plants epiphytic (Sect. *Harpophyllae*)..................................go to 2
1. Stems thickened, pseudobulbous, plants rupicolous..... go to 4
2. Sepals and petals yellow.....................*Laelia brevicaulis*
2. Sepals and petals orange ....go to 3
3. Midlobe of lip straplike, narrow to tip, flowers bright orange ....*L. harpophylla*
3. Midlobe of lip widened at tip, flowers orange at maturity, yellow when opening...................*L. kautskyana*
4. Flowers red, orange or yellow...........................go to 5
4. Flowers pink, lavender or rosy or salmon-purple, though lip may be yellow or have red, yellow or white markings......go to 21
5. Flower stalk exceeding height of leaf 2–4 times (Sect. *Parviflorae*) ....go to 6
5. Flower stalk about same height as leaf, a little shorter or longer (Sect. *Esalqueanae*)...................................go to 19
6. Flowers concolor with orange-red sepals and petals ...*L. milleri*
6. Flowers otherwise ....go to 7
7. Sepals and lateral petals orange ....go to 8
7. Sepals and petals yellow...............................go to 11
8. Petals 25 mm. or more long...........................go to 9
8. Petals less than 25 mm. long.......................*L. angereri*
9. Lateral lobes of lip orange ....go to 10
9. Lateral lobes of lip red.........................*L. sanguiloba*
10. Flowers concolor orange, midlobe not stalked...............................*L. flava var. aurantiaca*
10. Flowers white or cream in throat, midlobe stalked ....*L. cinnabarina*
11. Midlobe of lip with distinct stalk before widening for apex..go to 12
11. Midlobe expanding from its base, not stalked ....go to 13
12. Petals 20–25 mm. long.........................*L. bahiensis*
12. Petals 30 mm. long ....*L. mixta*
13. Pseudobulbs less than 3 cm. high, flowers pale yellow ....*L. cardimii*
13. Pseudobulbs higher, 5 or more cm. high ....go to 14
14. Petals wide for their short length, 8–9 × 25 mm., with blunt or rounded tips ....*L. briegeri*
14. Petals not so wide for their length, narrower, usually more pointed..go to 15
15. Flowers bunched toward end of stalk..................*L. flava*
15. Flowers spaced along stalk, opening in sequence......go to 16
16. Stalk slender and bending, flowers pale yellow.......*L. gracilis*
16. Stalk more upright, flowers bright yellow ....go to 17
17. Petals to 20 mm. long..............................go to 18
17. Petals longer, 25 mm......................... *L. gloedeniana*
18. Lip midlobe a long elliptic shape ....*L. blumenscheinii*
18. Lip midlobe ovate or circular in shape ....*L. endsfeldzii*

19. Pseudobulbs short, drum-shaped, plants only 6–8 cm. high, petals less than 15 mm. long . . . . *L. bradei*
19. Pseudobulbs more pear-shaped, plants somewhat higher, petals 15 mm. or more long . . . . go to 20
20. Petals and sepals about 5–6 mm. wide . . . . *L. esalqueana*
20. Petals and sepals less wide, about 3–5 mm . . . . *L. itambana*
21. Flower stalk exceeding leaf height 2–4 times (Sect. *Rupestres*) . . . . go to 22
21. Flower stalk about the same as leaf in height, a little shorter or taller (Sect. *Liliputanae*) . . . . go to 29
22. Flowers with all yellow lip, ... *L. gardneri*
22. Flowers with lips purple, purple and white or purple and yellow . . . . go to 23
23. Lip with short stiff pubescence in throat area, lip pointed . . . . *L. hispidula*
23. Lip without pubescence, rounded or indented at tip . . . go to 24
24. Flowers 3–5 crowded at apex of stalk . . . . *L. crispata*
24. Flowers usually more numerous, spaced along the stalk . . . . go to 25
25. Flowers small, petals to 20–25 mm. long . . . . go to 26
25. Flowers larger, petals around 30–35 mm. long . . . . go to 27
26. Lip elongated, when spread flat almost twice as long as broad . . . . *L. caulescens*
26. Lip about equal in width and length . . . . *L. pfisteri*
27. Lip midlobe stalked before it expands . . . . *L. crispilabia*
27. Midlobe expanding directly, not stalked . . . . go to 28
28. Plants distinctly glaucous having a grey-green color . . . . *L. tereticaulis*
28. Plants usual dark green with red flushes on reverse of leaf . . . . *L. mantiqueirae*
29. Lip yellow, sometimes veined with purple or having a rosy flush along edges . . . . go to 30
29. Lip purple with white or yellow in throat . . . . go to 31
30. Petals about 20–22 mm. long . . . . *L. lucasiana*
30. Petals about 13–15 mm. long . . . . *L. reginae*
31. Pedicel and ovary extra long, about 3–5 cm. . . . . go to 32
31. Pedicel and ovary about 2–3 cm. or less long, about . . . go to 33
32. Pointed flower parts, yellow in throat of lip . . . . *L. longipes*
32. Rounded flower segments, white to cream in throat . . . . *L. duveenii*
33. Column distinctly winged or edged toward its base . . . . . *L. ghillanyi*
33. Column not winged or edged . . . . go to 34
34. Flower concolor lavender pink, flower stalk sheath only 8 mm. high . . . . *L. liliputana*
34. Flower with distinct yellow on lip, sheath 10 mm. or more high . . . . *L. kettieana*

TABLE VI

Lip sizes of the Subgenus *Parviflora* species of *Laelia*. All measurements in millimeters, made from actual flowers or taken from type descriptions

Section *Harpophyllae*
brevicaulis	15 × 30
harpophylla	17 × 30
kautskyana	14 × 21

Section *Parviflorae*
angereri	12 × 20
bahiensis	13 × 17
blumenscheinii	11 × 15
briegeri	15 × 17
cardimii	8 × 8
cinnabarina	15 × 35
endsfeldzii	10 × 14
flava	16 × 24
gloedeniana	14 × 19
gracilis	10 × 14
milleri	12 × 18
mixta	14 × 20
sanguiloba	12 × 22

Section *Esalqueanae*
bradei	9.5 × 11
esalqueana	9 × 10
itambana	10 × 11

Section *Rupestres*
caulescens	10 × 16
crispata	12 × 17
crispilabia	12 × 15
gardneri	8 × 12
hispidula	12 × 14
mantiqueirae	14 × 17
pfisteri	10 × 14
tereticaulis	12 × 14

Section *Liliputanae*
duveenii	15 × 15
ghillanyi	14 × 12
kettieana	11 × 13
liliputana	8 × 8
longipes	14 × 15
lucasiana	14 × 14
reginae	9 × 7

TABLE VII

Fieldmarks for Quick Recognition of the Subgenus
Parviflorae species of *Laelia*

Harpophyllae—thin stems, orange or yellow flowers
    brevicaulis—yellow flowers, narrow pointed midlobe
    harpophylla—brillant orange, narrow strap-like midlobe
    kautskyana—midlobe expanded at tip, paler orange flowers
        opening yellow then darkening
Parviflorae—enlarged pseudobulbous stems, yellow, orange or
    red flowers on tall stalks above leaves
    angereri—tallest plants, orange flowers clustered at top of
        stalk
    bahiensis—stalked midlobe, intense deep yellow, flowers
        spaced on stalk opening one after the other
    blumenscheinii—small flowers, elliptic shaped midlobe,
        flowers spaced at top of stalk
    briegeri—wide petals for length, bright yellow, good to fine
        form, up to 5 flowers on tall stalk
    cardimii—small plants, 3–4 pale yellow flowers, darker
        yellow lips
    cinnabarina—largest flowers, orange, ruffled stalked
        midlobe
    endsfeldzii—small pale yellow flowers, red inside on base of
        lip, rugose leaves, flowers spaced along stalk
    flava—clustered flowers at top of stalk, good form, concolor
        yellow, necked pseudobulbs, concolor orange variety
        rare
    gloedeniana—medium-sized flowers, red veins on yellow
        lip, flowers spaced on stalk
    gracilis—bending tall stalk, pale yellow flowers
    milleri—red-orange flowers
    mixta—can be yellow or salmony color, stalked midlobe
    sanguiloba—starry, orange flowers except for distinctly red
        lateral lobes of the lip
Esalqueanae—small plants with yellow flowers appearing shorter
    than or scarcely above height of leaf
    bradei—tiniest plants of all yellows, wide segments, lemon
        yellow, 2–3 flowers, drum-shaped pseudobulbs
    esalqueana—wide petals, 3–4 flowers, variable
    itambana—small narrow flower segments, 1–2 flowers, long
        ovary
Rupestres—pseudobulbous, tall flower stalks with purple flowers
    caulescens—medium size flowers, lip twice as long as broad,
        flowers spaced at tip of stalk
    crispata—crowded flowers, deep yellow on disc, winter-
        flowering here (old *rupestris*)
    crispilabia—stalked midlobe, white on disc, pale rangy
        flowers; plants reman green
    gardneri—yellow lip, but plants not as dwarf as other
        yellow-lipped species
    hispidula—off-purple color, pointed lip, hispid inner lip
        surface
    mantiqueirae—white on disc of medium-sized flower
    pfisteri—small, spaced-apart flowers, white on disc
    tereticaulis—glaucous plants without red flushes, flowers
        similar to *crispata* but spring-flowering here, sepals
        and petals usually recurved

Liliputanae—tiny plants with heavy succulent leaves, purple
         flowers on short stalks

     duveenii—intense color, crystalline texture, long ovary,
            rounded petals and sepals, white in throat

     ghillanyi—winged column especially toward its base

     kettieana—yellow disc with deep magenta border around
            lip

     liliputanae—smallest plants of all rock species, almost no
            flower stalk sheath, single flowers, rounded
            pseudobulbs

     longipes—pedicel and ovary long, but flower stalk short

     lucasiana—bright yellow lip, plants without red flushes (old
            ostermayeri)

     reginae—yellow lip with purple flushes, petals pinky
            lavender, rounded tips on sepals and petals

Section *Harpophyllae*

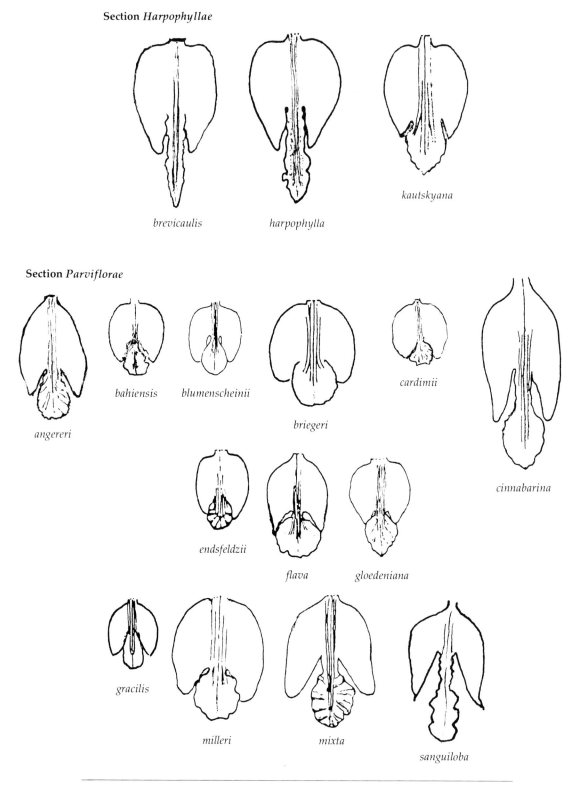

Fig. 2. Lip outlines of the rock laelias, Subgenus *Parviflorae*. Scale relative; not exact.

Section *Esalqueanae*

bradei *esalqueana* *itambana*

Section *Rupestres*

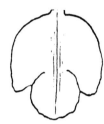
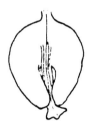
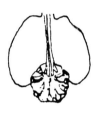

caulescens *crispata* *crispilabia* *gardneri* *hispidula*

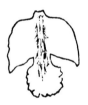

mantiqueirae *pfisteri* *tereticaulis*

Section *Liliputanae*

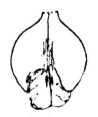

duveenii *ghillanyi* *kettieana* *liliputana* *longipes*

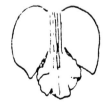

lucasiana *reginae*

CHAPTER 2

Description of Species

List of species

Fig. 8. *Laelia anceps.* A light-colored Guerrero form. Photo by Paul Gripp.

single leaf, rarely two, is produced. The leaves are oblong-lanceolate, of heavy texture, 15–20 cm. long and of a light green color. The flower stalk rises to as much as 3 ft. (almost 1 m.) and bears up to five flowers. The starry, well-held flowers are about 4 in. (10 cm.) across, some smaller. The sepals and petals are usually a bright rose-purple with the lip a dark rich reddish purple. The throat is lighter in color on the sides and white centrally with radiating purple lines. There may be a definite yellow patch on the disc, or the white of the throat may be accentuated. Three central thickened veins form a callus that is bright yellow in color, and it terminates on the disc in either the yellow or white area.

The idea of splitting this species into various others is not new. In 1902 de Barri Crawshay proposed (*Gard. Chron.* 3rd s., 32:44) after many years of careful study that the varieties *dawsonii, hollidayana, sanderiana, schroederae* and *schroederiana* be raised to species status. He listed various subvarieties, except for *dawsonii* that stood by itself, to be included under each of these taxa, with 59 remaining named forms to be included in *L. anceps* proper. So far as I know, the precise differences among these forms was never published by Crawshay, nor was the idea developed beyond the listing stage.

Since several of the named clones from years ago are still grown—or at least plants with such varietal labels are known—it would seem sensible to describe several in order to straighten out possible confusion. Veitch classifies some of these as "subvarieties", differing only in color from the type forms; others he accords full varietal status; and later orchidists have called them "sub-species". Some will undoubtedly coordinate with the new research in México. There is an original list of the varieties in the Feb., 1896, *Orchid Review*, and again in the Jan., 1922 issue. The following reflects Crawshay's ideas.

'Dawsonii' has larger than average flowers, was the first form with white sepals and petals, appearing in T. Dawson's collection at Meadow Bank, Glasgow, Scotland, and was described in 1868. The lip was white, streaked thickly with red-purple veinings in the throat, and with the midlobe a rich purple edged in white. It was noted in the 1922 article that many plants had come from the original area near Cordoba and all were called 'Dawsonii', the name not indicating a specific clone. Crawshay said in 1902 that the idea that they were all grown from one plant was an error. The original plant was found by John Tucker near Juquila, México.

'Hollidayana' had a crimson midlobe and veining in the throat, instead of the usual dark red-purple, a shorter, broader lip and was equivalent to varieties 'Ashworthiana' (a slate blue form), 'Simondsii', 'Waddoniensis', and 'White Queen'.

'Sanderiana' is similar to 'Dawsonii' but with smaller, narrower sepals and petals, and the lip shows some purple in the veins, a rose-purple blotch on the front lobe, less yellow on the keels and is otherwise white. It was described in 1885 and was found with plants called 'Stella'. These had flowers with the same lack of coloration but had broader proportions in all parts. They came from the Pacific Coast areas.

'Schroederae', or Baroness Schroeder', described in 1887, was a satiny rose with purple tips on sepals and petals, and the midlobe deep maroon-purple toward its apex. This was con-sidered equivalent to the following varieties: 'Amesiana', 'Ballantineana', 'Crawshayana', and 'Theodora'.

'Schroederiana', named in 1885, was distinct in the large, full form of both the petals, the lip and the color of the flower. It was white, and the only color was in the lines of purple in the throat.

The so-called subvarieties of *L. anceps* proper would include the following forms, among others, distinguished on the basis of color varia-tion from the usual, also peloria:

'Alba' or 'Virginalis', white flowers with yellow only on the disc of the lip. Also 'Bull's Alba' and 'Worthington's Alba' belong here.

'Blanda', with white sepals and the petals a light rose flush, the side lobes rose-purple and the midlobe deep purple.

'Hilliana', sepals and petals nearly white, the lip bordered with light rose. From the Gulf side.

'Holocheila', a distinctive peloric form with the lip like a petal; rosy lilac throughout.

'Percivaliana', with white sepals and rose-purple petals, the lateral lobes of the lip tipped in amethyst-purple. From the Gulf side.

'Roeblingiana' is another peloric form with the petals looking like the lip and colored in crimson-purple.

'Rosea', from the Gulf side, white delicately tinted with rose, especially on the lip.

'Veitchiana', with bluish instead of lavender markings. This cultivar, presumably all divisions of the original clone, has been given two HCC's and one AM by the AOS. Once again, we have confusion over what is indicated by a varietal name in the orchid world—or were these really awards for good culture of the plant? Although new blue cultivars may have been found by now, or the original clone may have been selfed to raise new seedlings in captivity, the author does not yet know of it.

Other varieties have been singled out for larger-than-ordinary size or for superior coloring, and several authors made note of the white midrib area at the base of the petals—not an attractive feature in the eyes of most judges. Of more recent date than these older forms is the 'Irwin' AM/AOS clone with larger, darker flowers, the natural spread running 14.6 cm. Also of note is the 'San-Bar Gloriosa' FCC/AOS clone with flowers measuring 12 cm. across and remarkably colored, with sepals lighter than petals, a glowing rosy lavender, and much yellow prominent on the disc. This clone is an outstanding example of the Guerrero taxon mentioned above. Hybridizers, using the peloric 'Roeblingiana', have noted a new and intense rosy coloration of both sepals and petals in the offspring, an unexpected bonus.

The culture of *L. anceps* cannot be better described than in the following quote from an account of Kienast-Zolly, who lived for many years in México and later grew orchids in Zurich. His account was published in the *Gardeners' Chronicle* for 1887, p. 413.

This orchid is always met with on the borders of the virgin forest, growing on the trunks of trees, and on the very slender branches exposed to a powerful sun and to strong winds; often also clinging to rocks covered with the remains of leaves and moss under the same conditions. During the rainy season, from May to October, these plants are daily drenched by torrents of rain of which they experience the full force, often for five consecutive hours, and are thoroughly wet throughout the night. About 6 a.m, a sharp and fresh wind coming from the highest peaks of the Cordilleras, many of which are capped with perpetual snow, begins to dry the plants—a work which the burning sun completes—pitilessly shining on them for several hours, until the daily storm drenches them afresh. Under these conditions *Laelia anceps* grows with extraordinary vigor, and flowers about the end of October, or in November, just as the new pseudo-bulbs arrive at their perfect development. About

Fig. 9. *Laelia anceps* 'Tara'. Oaxaca form. Photo by Trudi Marsh.

the end of February, new roots start from the base of the bulb—
this is the time of the short rainy season, called the Golden Rain
of the coffee planters—the fine rain falling almost like a fog; this
rain is too weak to saturate the plants, it is hardly able to refresh
them, so that the rest is scarcely interrupted by it. The pseudobulbs of plants fully exposed to the sun are always large, hard,

and of a reddish colour, the leaves leathery and broad; whilst those plants which grow more in the shade have longer and thinner bulbs and leaves.

Many hybrids have been produced with *L. anceps* over the years. Its stately bearing, starry shape with elongated pointed petals, and its elongated flower stalk are usually dominant in most combinations, as is the lip coloration and configuration. The species and its varieties well deserve their long popularity. It should be noted that when crossed with *L. cinnabarina* to produce *L.* Ancibarina, a Colman cross from 1914, the flowers are orange in color. Whether this indicates a likely dominance of the orange pigmentation of the *cinnabarina* over the purple color of the *anceps* will not really be known until someone can tell us what form of *anceps* was used in the hybridization. For those interested in the breeding behavior of laelias, this could be a critical point.

One of the first hybrids noted was *L. finckeniana*, a natural hybrid described in 1885 between a white form of *anceps* and *L. albida*. The plant had been chosen by Fincken because of its distinctive appearance from an imported lot of *L. anceps*, coming from the Pacific side of México, made by the Liverpool Horticultural Co. It has since been remade in cultivation. The hybrid, *L. crawshayana*, is presumably the same thing. Hybrid plants produced in cultivation are properly named *L.* Finckeniana. Natural hybrids of *anceps* with *autumnalis* or with *furfuracea* are not reported. In California a plant called *L. ashworthii* is being cultivated. It appears to be a hybrid, but at present I cannot find out more about it, and it may not involve *L. anceps* at all.

Angerer's Laelia

Brazil

Laelia angereri Pabst. 1975. *Orchid Digest* 39 (4):153.
Subgenus: *Parviflorae*
Section: *Parviflorae*

According to Duveen and Fowlie, the brick-red or orange color of the flowers of this species makes it easy to spot. It has floral segments of medium width, in proportion to their length, and the petals are blunt, the sepals somewhat pointed. The sepals may have a whitish area at their bases.

The tube of the lip as it covers the column is curved, and the colored veins are easily seen on the pale yellow outer surface of the base of the lip. The veining is also prominent on the midlobe, as the veins emerge from the throat onto the pale yellow disc. The edges of the midlobe are much waved, and the tip reflexes back like *L. cinnabarina*, with which this species is closely related. The midlobe appears to have a short but definite isthmus at its origin—according to the type description. We need to study more live plants in cultivation of this species as well as other rupicolous species to understand better their range of variation in anatomical details.

The petals are a little longer than the dorsal sepal. The measurements by Duveen and Fowlie are: sepals 14–22 mm. long × 4.5 mm. wide, and petals 15–22 mm. long × 4.5 mm. wide. This is a comparatively broad width for these flower parts for a plant related closely to *cinnabarina*. From the drawing, the lip is 11–12 mm. wide and 20 mm. long. There is little other quantitative data available for these plants, but they are well illustrated in their habitat in *Native Orchids of Brasil*.

Pseudobulbs on wild plants measure 34–35 cm. tall, are thickened at the base, and the leaves add another 30 cm. to the height. The stiff and channeled leaves are about 3 cm. wide, dark green with a deep red flush and have a roughened surface. The flower stalk reaches to 30–35 cm., and there may be from 5–15 flowers tightly grouped toward the apex. In Brazil they flower from July to September and grow from 1000–1200 m.

This species is found northeast of the Diamantina region in the state of Minas Gerais in central Brazil. The species is named after Ernesto Angerer, who discovered the plants while collecting in an out-of-the-way area of the Serra do Mané Pinheiro in 1971. It is obviously one of the tallest of the rupicolous laelias, in company with *L. blumenscheinii*, and in cultivation flowers in the spring.

Pabst was of the opinion that *L. hispidula* was a natural hybrid of *L. angereri* and *L. crispata*, but this is not confirmed. Since *L. hispidula* is only described and illustrated in a watercolor, its identity will remain in doubt until further field work, or hybridization in cultivation, can clear up this situation.

Fig. 10. *Laelia angereri.*

Fig. 11. *Laelia autumnalis.* Dark form comparable to 'Atrorubens'. Photo by Paul Gripp.

Autumn-flowering Laelia

México

Laelia autumnalis (Llav. and Lex.) Lindley. 1831. *Gen. and Sp. Orch. Plants,*
p. 115
      Subgenus: *Laelia*
        Section: *Podolaelia*

Synonyms
Bletia autumnalis (Lindley) Llav. and Lex. 1825. Llave and Lexarza's *Nov.*
   Veg. Descr. 2: Orch. Opusc. 2:19.
Cattleya autumnalis Beer. 1854. *Prak. Stud. Fam. Orch.,* p. 208.

This autumn-flowering laelia from México blooms in cultivation from
December through January in more northerly locations. But, according to
some orchidists, the species may be a complex of two or more types based
on the degree to which the sepals and petals are reflexed at their tips and
whether the tips are green or the more usual purple-red color.

For one of these isolates, refer to the description of *L. bancalarii,* a
species with a different flowering season and a distribution toward the

Pacific in western Jalisco and Nayarit. Otherwise, *L. autumnalis* is to be found with a wide distribution in the mountains of several states from Oaxaca in the south to Sonora and Chihuahua in the north.

The pseudobulbs are more or less ovoid, distinctly ridged, and bear two, sometimes even three, stiff, pointed narrow leaves that are a gray-green, often tinged with maroon, especially when the plant grows in an exposed position. The plants are very tough and hardy, grow high in the mountains, often on scrubby oaks, sometimes on mossy rocks, and are well suited to the severe dormancy, coolness, and bright light to which they are exposed. In this respect they are similar to the other laelias in the *Podolaelia* section, all of which tolerate similar habitat niches under full force of sun and rain (see habitat description under *L. anceps*). Well established plants can form large masses of pseudobulbs clumped tightly together around the branches.

The pseudobulbs may reach 2–6 in. (up to 15 cm.) in height, and the leaves are another 11–16 cm. (to 6–7 in.) long. The dark maroon upright flower stalk is up to 18–24 in. high (to 25 cm.), is tightly covered with bracts, and can bear as many as 13–15 flowers, though 5 or 6 are more common. The flowers vary from a pink to a deep red-purple, and white forms also have been found. The blossoms are about 3 in. (8 cm.) across, but some report widths of up to 10–15 cm. The latter would be a remarkable size and certainly tops for this species. The white lateral lobes of the lip are a distinctive feature of these flowers, and the keels are yellow.

The plants were first reported in cultivation in 1836 by Tayleur, of Parkfield, near Liverpool, then by Barker of Birmingham. Both Loddiges and Stuart Low and Co., and then others, imported quantities of this species so that it was generally available. In México, since it flowers at the end of October, it is called *Flor de Todos los Santos* (All Saints' Flower), and at that time it is available in large bouquets in the local markets. The flower spikes are pulled from the plants, often with the lead growth attached, to give the flowers nourishment so they last well. This causes two or three older bulbs to sprout new growths, so the process is not as devastating to the natural population as it might seem.

Two or three varietal forms have been described in addition to the alba white forms, in particular one called 'Atrorubens' with larger flowers than ordinary of a brilliant crimson-purple and with petal tips and the top of the column a darker hue. Variety 'Venusta', by contrast, was a uniform rosy mauve.

Hybrids are not well known, but in nature the plants often grow in proximity to *L. furfuracea*, and *L. autumnalis* var. *xanthotropis*, introduced by Sander, was thought by Reichenbach to be a combination of those two. The idea was strengthed by the observation that the plant flowered in July-August rather than October or later. It is characterized by smaller, shorter leaves, very broad petals, pale rose color and the lip wider and shorter than usual. These characteristics certainly seem intermediate between the two species, but the hybrid still lacks a formally published name. The plant is being grown today in California and elsewhere as *L. xanthotropis*, as though it were a species. Writing it as *L. Xanthotropis* would be more accurate by the present Rules, had the plants been produced in cultivation and registered with the R.H.S.

Laelia eyermaniana, named by Reichenbach in 1888, was a presumed natural hybrid between *L. autumnalis* and *L. speciosa,* and since then has been considered to be *L. albida* × *L. speciosa.* Little is known about it today.

Fig. 12. *Laelia autumnalis* var. *xanthotropis.* Photo by Trudi Marsh.

Fig. 13. *Laelia bahiensis.*

Bahia Laelia

Brazil

Laelia bahiensis Schlechter. 1921. *Fedde Repert. Spec. Nov.* 17:272.
Subgenus: *Parviflorae*
Section: *Parviflorae*

This is a golden-yellow flowered species, and the flowers open one
after another on a tall stalk above the leaves. It comes from the Serra da
Sincorá Mountains in Bahia, from which its name is derived. It has also
been collected in the Serra do Calabocária and the Serra do Capa-Bode.
From the time of its original discovery until 1972, when it was rediscovered, its location was unknown.

The pseudobulbs are from 4–7 cm. high and are up to 1.8 mm. in
diameter across their bulbous bases, with a leaf 6.5–8 cm. high and 1.5–2
cm. wide. In cultivation, the sizes of growths and leaves may increase as a

result of less intense light. Measurement of a well-grown plant showed leaves 2.5 cm. × 10.5 cm. Young growths may be bifoliate. The mature growths are a dark deep green, usually rugose, and have a red flush both on the pseudobulbs and the backs of the leaves.

The flower stalk can reach 70 cm., though usually half that size, and bears 4–8 flowers at the top which are produced in sequence. The sheath is 4.2 cm. long, and the stalk has four nodes. The flowers in cultivation are medium-sized for this group with the sepals measuring about 24 mm. and the petals 25 mm., both about 6 mm. wide. They have a crystalline texture in the sun, and the deep yellow petals show some red veining. The lip measures 17 mm. long by 13 mm. wide. The oval midlobe has a ruffled upturned margin, and the disc is a pale white extending from the throat with red veins showing upon it. The outside of the lateral lobes is white with red veining, and the lobes show deep yellow at their tips. The column is marked with red and yellow flushes and has a white anther cap.

These flowers are similar in appearance to those of *L. endsfeldzii*, also of this section, but that species is somewhat smaller-flowered, a paler lemon yellow, has less ruffling of the lip margin, and the proportions of the lateral lobes and midlobe are different when the lip is flattened for study (see Fig. 2).

As is the case with the rupicolous laelias, little is known of the specifics for cultivation other than the general rules for a rock laelia. This one flowers in April and May in the northern hemisphere, in September through November in Brazil. It was originally collected by Luetzelburg in Bahia without a more specific location.

Bancalari's Laelia

México

Laelia bancalarii Gonzalez, Tamayo and Hagsater. 1984. *Orquidea* (Mex.) 9: 366, fig.
      Subgenus: *Laelia*
        Section: *Podolaelia*

This taxon was recently named as a separate species from the complex of forms around *L. autumnalis*. It grows mostly on oaks at 1000 m. or more on the Pacific slopes of western Jalisco where it is apparently endemic. One of the easy distinctions is that it flowers in México in February to April, not the October–December season of *L. autumnalis*. We could expect it to flower in early summer in more northerly greenhouse locations.

According to the descriptions, the two leaves are somewhat longer and narrower than those of *autumnalis*, up to 25 cm. long × 2.5 cm. wide, and the slightly larger flowers have a more compact arrangement. The petals and sepals are up to 6–7 cm. long, and the petals may be 3 cm. wide. The tips of the petals often recurve. The usual color of the flowers is rose-purple, but it can be pink. The inside of the lateral lobes is flushed with darker red-purple, with white outside, and the three callus keels are the

Fig. 14. *Laelia bancalarii.* Photo by Raymond McCullough.

usual yellow. The long flower stalk may bear 6 or 7 flowers.

We still know nothing of this species in cultivation, but its culture would parallel the other Méxican species of this section. The species is named for Dr. Carlos Bancalari Rodriguez (1906–1973), who first discovered the plants and called them to the Méxican orchidologists' attention.

Blumenschein's Laelia

Brazil

Laelia blumenscheinii Pabst. 1975. *Bradea* 1 (50):487, fig.
    Subgenus: *Parviflorae*
        Section: *Parviflorae*

It is appropriate that Blumenschein be honored with a namesake *Laelia* since he, as a student of Brieger, did so much research and field work on the rupicolous species.

The pseudobulbs of these plants are somewhat elongated and measure up to 12–15 cm. high, and the roughened (rugose) leaves add another 17 cm., with a width of about 3 cm. They are dark green with a red flush. The spathe measures 5.6 cm. in our specimen.

This is another species with a tall flower stalk, up to 38 cm. tall, or even higher, and it may have five nodes. Held well above the leaves, there are 5–7 to 10–12 flowers tightly clustered at the end of the stalk. They are light citron yellow with brownish veining in the throat. The midlobe of the lip is somewhat elongated, four-nerved on the disc, slightly ruffled on the edges

Fig. 15. *Laelia blumenscheinii.* Photo by Trudi Marsh.

and recurved at the tip. The plant also occurs in an *alba* form. The leaves of these *alba* plants are all green with no reddish pigmentation.

The dorsal sepal measures 5 mm. × 16 mm., the lateral sepals slightly larger and slightly curved. The petals are 5.5 mm. wide × 20 mm. long. In some specimens the flowers have narrower sepals and petals. The lip is broadly elliptic when flattened for study and measures 15 mm. long by 11 mm. broad. It shows a distinctly stalked midlobe.

The plants were found in Espírito Santo, near Pequiá, by the Baron Anton de Ghillány. In Brazil they flower in April–May. Hamilton's data indicate January–February flowering in cultivation in northern locations.

Brade's Laelia

Brazil

Laelia bradei Pabst. 1973. *Bradea* 1 (31): 332.
Subgenus: *Parviflorae*
Section: *Esalqueanae*

This species belongs to the small group whose plants have yellow flowers and a flower stalk not much higher than the leaves. It is the smallest of the rock-dwelling laelias with pale yellow flowers, but even so, the sepals and petals are relatively broad in their proportions. The lip is somewhat crisped. The plants flower from December–January in Brazil.

The small, dumpy plants have short 2–4 cm. pseudobulbs that are squat and drum-shaped, nearly as thick as tall. The very fleshy, stiff leaves are short and strongly channeled or cupped along the midribs, almost boat-shaped, and are 1.4 cm. wide × 3–4 cm. long. The plants are not more than 6–8 cm. high and distinctive in appearance even out of bloom. They are green or red depending upon their exposure on the lichen-covered rocks where they grow in cracks and crevices.

The scape measures 5–6 cm. from a sheath that is only about .5 cm. long. There may be three flowers. Dorsal sepals measure 4 × 16 mm.; petals are the same size. The lip flattened measures 9.5 mm. broad × 11 mm. long. Though the flowers are small, they tend to have a full shape.

The limited distribution is near Diamantina in the state of Minas Gerais at about 1300 m. altitude. The species is also described from Espírito Santo at about 1200 m. The type specimen was collected by A. C. Brade after whom the species was named.

Fig. 16. *Laelia bradei.* Photo by Trudi Marsh.

Fig. 17. *Laelia brevicaulis.*

Short-stalked Laelia

Brazil

Laelia brevicaulis (H. G. Jones) Withner *comb. nov..*
    Basionym: *Hoffmannseggella brevicaulis* H. G. Jones
    Subgenus: *Parviflorae*
        Section: *Harpophyllae*

Synonyms
Laelia cowanii Hort. 1898. Catalogue of Messrs. John Cowan and Co.,
    Gateacre Nurseries. Cited in *Orchid Rev.* 6 (72): 376. Further cita-
    tions 8 (87):78 and 8 (88):122–123.
Laelia cowanii Hort. 1898. Cited by A. Cogniaux in *Chron. Orch. suppl.*
    Dict. Icon.:172.
Hoffmannseggella brevicaulis H. G. Jones. 1972. *Rhodora* 74: 283–286.

This species, according to the information published in various citations, has been confused with both *L. harpophylla* and *L. kautskyana*, also
with *L. cinnabarina*, but it is nevertheless a distinct population. This is the
only yellow-flowered taxon in the *Harpophyllae* section with its epiphytic
species. The *brevicaulis* name refers to the flower stalk, shorter than the
leaves.

In my experience, it has distinctly different flowers and coloration when compared to *kautskyana*. Though *kautskyana* is sometimes described as "yellow", the flowers are in reality pale orange at maturity, certainly not the golden yellow of this species. Also, the shape of the lobes of the lip is different, as well as the sepals and petals

Additional confusion arises with the name *cowanae* (*cowanii, cowani*) that seems in past years to have been attached as a variety to *L. cinnabarina*—for no real reason except a lack of accurate knowledge about its true identity and how the word was spelled. No one with a plant so labeled has ever been able to tell me what really made it different from typical *L. cinnabarina*. Usually there was some suggestion that the flowers were smaller—or larger!

Research done for this volume shows that the *cowanii* epithet was a catalog designation never validly published as a species, nor was a herbarium specimen or illustration of it ever prepared. Rolfe, writing in the *Orchid Review*, said the "*cowani*" plants had long slender pseudobulbs, 6–9 in. (15–25 cm.), and narrow leaves the same length, similar to those of *L. harpophylla*. The lip was described as recurved and the flowers golden yellow. Not recognizing it as a new species, Rolfe speculated on its parentage as a possible natural hybrid: *flava/harpophylla* or *harpophylla/cinnabarina*.

These plants, since they had the appearance of *L. harpophylla*, were also sometimes called the yellow *harpophylla*. So the confusion continued to build, and the name was used without regard to its original purpose. In 1972 Jones published the epithet of *Hoffmannseggella brevicaulis* for a yellow laelia he found while studying at the Reichenbach Herbarium in Vienna. Unfortunately, he did not describe or designate the identity of those specimen sheets there and declared the type to be in his own herbarium in Barbados, prepared from a plant under cultivation in his collection. No connection was made by Jones with the information available on *L. cowanii*, but I find that the information on the two coincides without problems.

In the type description of *H. brevicaulis* the flowers are described as 6.5 cm. across with sepals 9 mm. × 3.5 cm., the petals similar. The lip measures 1.5 cm. broad × 3 cm. long, has two keels, and the midlobe is narrowly attenuate, ending in a point. The midlobe of the lip is shorter and broader than that of *harpophylla* that has a long, narrow strap-like lip, and the flowers are yellow instead of red-orange. Also, it flowers a month later than its companion species, July–August in Brazil, instead of June–July.

We obviously need more specimens of this species for greater familiarization in cultivation, but at present none of the orchid nurseries in Brazil seem to know anything about it. And yet, over the years, it is obvious that several plants have turned up in collections. Figure 17 is a photo I took many years ago at the Brooklyn Botanic Garden of a plant that came to us from Brazil labeled *L. harpophylla* var. *flava*. It is possible that these plants may turn out to be color mutants of *harpophylla* or *kautskyana*, or hybrids, and do not deserve species status. However, I tend to doubt those hypotheses. They may have come from a limited area that has been cleared or burned and are therefore now extinct! The options remain open for further study. Let us hope that additional plants will again be found.

Fig. 18. *Laelia briegeri.*
Photo by Trudi Marsh.

Brieger's Laelia

Brazil

Laelia briegeri Blumenschein. 1960. *Publ. Cient. Inst. Genetica, ESALQ* 1: 41.
      Subgenus: *Parviflorae*
          Section: *Parviflorae*

The long flower stem and bright, intensely yellow flowers with wide sepals and petals make this species easy to recognize. It was found near Serro in Minas Gerais at about 1100 m. in the area called Lápinha e Cabeça do Bernardo. It flowers there in November and December. Hamilton's data indicate May–June flowering in cultivation here. Blumenschein observes that it is a natural tetraploid species with 80 chromosomes, as distinct from the other rock laelias where the diploid number of 40 chromosomes is more common. Actually, he found two population groups. The one bearing smaller flowers had fewer chromosomes, 42, 44, and 48, but not the tetraploid 80. He wondered if they were really the same species but lumped the two populations together for purposes of classification.

Plants of *L. briegeri* have the tall flower stalks typical of this section. The pseudobulbs and leaves together are 17–20 cm. high, and the stalk can reach 27 cm. more with 3–5 flowers. The petals are 23–25 mm. long × 8–9 mm. wide; the dorsal sepal is 25–26 mm. long. The lip when spread flat measures 15 mm. wide × 17 mm. long, and there can be red areas on either side in the throat. Perhaps the ploidy accounts for the ample size of the sepals and petals.

A few crosses have already been made with this popular species, and the plant habit and flower shape dominate. The color, so far, seems also to come through well in the hybrids, with the lip picking up veining or color patterns from the other parent. *Epilaelia* Bussey (*Encyclia tampense alba* × *L. briegeri*) is particularly attractive, the long flower spike of the *briegeri* being dominant in the cross.

An *alba* form of the species has been found. Odebrecht (1988) observes that flowers of this species shade from creamy white to dark yellow-gold.

Cardim's Laelia

Brazil

Laelia cardimii Pabst and Mello. 1978. *Bradea* 2 (33): 225–230.
Subgenus: *Parviflorae*
Section: *Parviflorae*

This laelia is named after Flávio Cardim, the chief grower for many years at Orquidário Binot. It is pale yellow-flowered with 3–4 blooms on a tall, thin stem well exceeding the leaves. The lip is a darker yellow than the sepals and petals and may have a red flush at its base. There may also be a touch of red at the base and on the tips of the sepals and petals. The flowers and plants fit nicely into the section *Parviflorae* despite their small size compared to other species of that section. The leaves usually display a reddish color when exposed to good light.

This is the only yellow rupicolous laelia growing on the Serra do Cipó in Minas Gerais. The pseudobulbs measure 1.6–2.5 cm. high and the leaves are 4.6–7.5 cm. long on the same plants. The flower stalk is 11.3 cm. to the first of three flowers on my specimen. Occasional young growths produce two leaves, but mature growths have only one. The dorsal sepal measures 4 × 14 mm.; the petals 3 × 13 mm.; the lateral sepals 4.5 × 12 mm.; and the lip is 8 mm. broad and the same length. The plant flowers in April and May in cultivation. The type description indicates flowers may be half again larger than the sizes reported here, with August flowering in Brazil.

Fig. 19. *Laelia cardimii* 'Hillside' CBR/AOS. Photo by Ron Parsons.

Fig. 20. *Laelia caulescens.*
Photo by Trudi Marsh.

Caulescent Laelia

Brazil

Laelia caulescens Lindley. 1841. *Bot. Reg.* 27, sub t. 1
    Subgenus: *Parviflorae*
        Section: *Rupestres*

Synonyms
Bletia caulescens Reichenbach f. 1861. *Walp. Ann. Bot.* 6: 431.
Bletia caulescens var. *libonis* Reichenbach f. 1863. *Xenia Orch.* 2:60.
Hoffmannseggella caulescens (Ldl.) Jones. 1970. *Caldasia* 10: 491–495.

There was some early confusion about this species as Lindley in *Bot. Reg.* 28, sub t. 62 (1842) reduced the name to a synonym under *L. flava.* Unfortunately, however, this species was described as having purple-violet flowers, and *L. flava* has only yellow blooms. In 1842 the variability and complexity of the rupicolous laelias was not yet understood, and pressed herbarium specimens did not always clearly show the color or details of flower structure. The *Orchid Digest* account of Pabst's research does include it in the key and text, but a picture is lacking. It is distinguished in the key by the lip being long and narrow when spread flat, twice as long as broad.

According to present thinking, this is probably a separate species related to *L. crispata* and does not have anything, of course, to do directly with *L. flava.* But we still are not certain of its actual status. In my opinion, it is likely to be the same as *L. mantiqueirae.* In that case, this name from 1841 would have the priority. They occur at the same altitude, grow in the same general region and may have the same lip configuration. Further field observations and better herbarium material could resolve this problem. Cunha Filho's research (1966) indicates a congener species to *crispilabia.*

The plant habit is medium in size with the pseudobulbs short, enlarged at the base, 3–8 cm. tall. The leathery leaf is somewhat concave and 6–12 cm. long. The flower stalk, as the name *caulescens* indicates, is taller than the leaves, and produces five or six well-spaced blooms. The lip is five-nerved, and the front edge is strongly crisped. The sepals are 2 cm. long with the dorsal about 2.5 mm. wide, the lateral 3–3.5 mm. The petals are 2 cm. long × 3 mm. wide, attenuate in shape. The lip is presumably 15–16 mm. long and 10–11 mm. wide, the column 7.5 mm. long.

The plant is illustrated clearly in *Martius' Flora Brasiliensis*, volume 3, part 6, plate 65, with accompanying text in part 5, from which the flower measurements above have been taken. The type specimen, which was in Martius' herbarium, was collected in the Serra da Piedade in Minas Gerais. Blumenschein also discusses this species in his thesis (1960), written before *mantiqueirae* was described, and notes it grows north of São João del Rei, between Itajubá and Belo Horizonte in Minas Gerais at about 950 m. altitude. It flowers between July and September in Brazil.

Blumenschein found that *L. caulescens* can be tetraploid with 80 instead of the usual 40 chromosomes common in this group. Also, he found that it was very close to *L. crispilabia* in the details of flower configuration, but reference to his drawings does not show the stalked midlobe that is distinctly indicated in Pabst's work on *crispilabia*. Both Blumenschein's

Fig. 21. *Laelia caulescens.*
Lip detail.
Photo by Trudi Marsh.

drawings and those in *Martius* by Cogniaux show the same non-stalked midlobes. Thus the confusion in the literature as to the specific identity of this species and its limits of variability continues.

Natural polyploidy has been noted in many orchids as well as other species of plants. It is usually associated with higher habitat altitudes or other "stressful" environments. Tetraploidy eventually acts to isolate a population reproductively from diploid congeners. If diploid clones of a population cross with tetraploid members of the same group, sterile triploids will be produced. But tetraploids may cross within their chromosome group, and eventually their offspring could form a separate species, spreading to ecological niches not suitable for diploid relatives. This process is undoubtedly a factor in both the number of species of rupicolous laelias now recognized, and it correlates with the strongly endemic distribution patterns characteristic of these rupicolous forms. Of the forms studied to date, the following have been shown to have natural tetraploid populations: *longipes, briegeri, rupestris* (now *crispata*), *caulescens, crispilabia* and *tereticaulis*.

Cinnabar Laelia

Brazil

Laelia cinnabarina Bateman *ex* Lindley. 1838. *Sertum Orchidaceum*, t. 28.
    Subgenus: *Parviflorae*
        Section: *Parviflorae*

Synonyms
Amalias cinnabarina (Bateman *ex* Lindley) Hoffmansegg. 1842. *Verz. Orch.* 37.
Cattleya cinnabarina (Bateman *ex* Lindley) Beer. 1854. *Prakt. Stud. Fam. Orch.*, p. 209.
Bletia cinnabarina (Bateman *ex* Lindley) Rchb. f. 1861. *Walp. Ann. Bot.* 6:430.
Bletia cinnabarina var. *sellowii* Reichenbach f. 1863. *Xenia Orch.* 2:61

The large, brilliant red-orange starry flowers of this laelia have attracted generations of orchid growers and have led to its repeated use in hybrids. The narrow, reflexed and much crisped lip with its narrow, midlobe isthmus is a dominant feature in its progeny. The firm tapered pseudobulbs, tightly covered with sheaths, stand clumped together, and the flower stalk can reach 40–50 cm. and produce as many as 10–12 flowers in sequence.

The pseudobulbs may reach 20–25 cm. while the leaves above measure 25–30 cm.—plants of this species are among the largest in its section. The flower parts are also large, in spite of belonging to the *Parviflorae*, with the dorsal sepal measuring 4–5 cm. long × 7–8 mm. wide, the petals of similar dimensions, the lateral sepals a little shorter. The lip is 2–3.5 cm. long × 12–15 mm. wide.

Plants were imported into England in 1836 from the southern parts of Minas Gerais and the adjacent state of Rio de Janeiro where they grew

Fig. 22. *Laelia cinnabarina.* Habitat in the Cerra do Caraca, Brazil.
Photo by Trudi Marsh.

upon rocks at around 800–1500 m. They were first exhibited in bloom by
Young of Epsom Nurseries in 1837 at the Royal Horticultural Society
meetings. The Hamilton Peak is March–May according to the numerous
records on this species.

The old cultural directions for growing this laelia in the cattleya
house—giving it all the light possible with no shade, except possibly
during the noon hours of summer—remain valid. It can be cultivated in
hanging baskets, on a slab, or in pots. Repotting is best done just after
flowering when the new growth begins. When well grown with proper
light, the plants take on a reddish hue that is a sign of good condition. Avoid
damaging or breaking the roots; they are critical in growing these
rupicolous laelias.

Fowlie and his co-researchers point out that in Brazil both cinnabar
and yellow forms of this species are distinguished. The larger, darker
orange types are called var. *cowanii*, but this is *not* a correct practice. That
name was never properly published, and in addition it was used for
describing a golden yellow species we now know as *L. brevicaulis* (please
see discussion there). If there is a true population of larger and darker
forms, or even yellow types of *L. cinnabarina*, they should be designated by
a new varietas name; otherwise, clonal designations for superior clones
should suffice. There is at this time no valid name for distinguishing sub-
populations of *L. cinnabarina*.

Among the many natural hybrids of *Laelia*, always a reflection of
which orchid species grow in proximity to one another in the wild, is one of
this species. It is *Lc. topaz*, a natural hybrid with *Cattleya warneri*. It was also
registered from production in cultivation by Charlesworth in 1901, and the

names of those plants would then be written *Lc.* Topaz. Another hybrid, presumed but not listed in Sanders' volumes, is *Lc.* Cinnamomea. Pabst and Dungs list it as a species, *L. cinnamomea*, but with no explanation or illustration, only the listing in the index. At this point it seems most likely to have been a clone of *cinnabarina* that was singled out for special attention and has not been heard of recently.

Fig. 23. *Laelia cinnabarina.* Lip detail. Photo by Trudi Marsh.

Crisped Laelia

Brazil

Laelia crispa Reichenbach f. 1853. *Flor. des Serres* series 1, 4:102
Subgenus: *Crispae*
Section: *Crispae*

Synonyms
Cattleya crispa Lindley. 1828. *Bot. Reg.* 14: t. 1172.
Cattleya reflexa Parmentier. 1861. *Walp. Ann. Bot.* 6:423.
Bletia crispa (Lindley) Rchb. f. 1861. *Walp. Ann. Bot.* 6: 423.

Named because all of the flower segments are much crisped, kinky or waved on the edges, this laelia is white with purple flushes except for the yellow in the throat and inside the tube of the lateral lobes of the lip and the amethyst-purple of the midlobe. The throat and the midlobe are both veined with a deeper purple, the reticulations being an attractive feature of the flower. The flower parts tend to be elongated, narrow, often twisted or reflexed, and with pointed tips, so that it has not been a favorite parent for the hybridizers. They have always preferred flat, fully formed flowers that do not have the dominant gyrations that usually show up in the progeny and must be bred out in subsequent generations. Nevertheless, a few hybrids with this species have been made.

This was one of the first laelias cultivated in England. Having been sent to the Horticultural Society of London in 1826 by Sir Henry Chamberlain, it flowered in the Horticultural Society greenhouses in August of 1827. The plants in nature grow on tall trees fully exposed to sun and air. They are occasionally found in massive clumps on rocks in the mountains at about 800–1000 m. in both Rio de Janeiro and neighboring Minas Gerais. Although originally described as a *Cattleya* by Lindley, it was placed in *Laelia* after the number of pollinia was found to be eight, a switch experienced by several other *Laelia* species.

The natural hybrid of *L. crispa* × *L. lobata (boothiana)* is called *L. wyattiana. Laelia lilacina* is the natural hybrid of *crispa* crossed with *perrinii*, and *Lc. delicata* is the hybrid with *C. forbesii.*

Fig. 24. *Laelia crispa* var. *delicatissima. Orchid Album* IX, plate 424, 1891.

Fig. 25. *Laelia crispa.*

Fig. 26. *Laelia crispata.*

Cliff-dwelling Laelia

Brazil

Laelia crispata (Thunb.) Garay. 1974. *Bradea* 1 (27): 302.
Subgenus: *Parviflorae*
Section: *Rupestres*

Synonyms

Cymbidium crispatum Thunberg. 1818. *Plantarum Braziliensium* 2: 18.
Laelia rupestris Lindley. 1842. *Bot. Reg.* 28, sub t. 62.
Bletia rupestris (Lindley) Reichenbach f. 1861. *Walp. Ann. Bot.* 6: 431.

This laelia has been known for years as *rupestris*, meaning rock- or cliff-dwelling in Latin, and not all orchidists today have changed their labels to read *crispata*. The R.H.S. still uses *rupestris* for the registration of hybrids of this species, so the duality will continue. We are used to that by now, trying to meld botanical knowledge and horticultural practice. Possible confusion is aggravated since *crispa*, *crispata* and *crispilabia* are three separate species contained in this genus.

As Pabst points out, *L. crispata* shares with *L. flava* and *L. cinnabarina* the characteristic of having one of the widest distributions of all the rupicolous laelias in Brazil. The plants are found in the mountains near Belo Horizonte in Minas Gerais and then north to Montes Claros, a distance of more than 500 km. The type specimen was collected near Diamantina in the Serra da Piedade. The plants grow at an altitude of 700–800 m., relatively low compared to other rock laelias, and Odebrecht (1988) describes collecting them en route to Diamantina from Rio de Janeiro.

The flowers are of medium size, about 4 cm. across with as many as ten produced in crowded succession on the apex of the flower stalk. They are easily recognized by their bright magenta color, the white bases of the sepals and petals, and the relatively broad width of the segments. The deep yellow in the throat spreads onto the base of the disc, and the apex of the lip is a darker red-purple than the sepals and petals. The midlobe is crisped as is typical for most of these rock laelia flowers. The sepals are 7–8 × 20 mm., the petals 7–8 × 21–22 mm., and the lip is 12–14 mm. broad × 16–17 mm. long. In Brazil the plants flower from September through December, in northerly climates mostly in February and March.

Two natural hybrids are reported by Pabst: one, a cross with *L. flava* and described under that species, is called *L. caetensis*; the other, described under *L. ghillanyi*, is called *L. cipoensis*. In cultivation the first hybrid was registered by Young in 1903, *Lc.* Glycera, using *C. trianaei* as the other parent. A variation named as a subspecies by Blum, *L. rupestris* subsp. *sanguinea*, presumably has flowers with a redder color than usual, and Blumenschein has shown the plants to be tetraploid. To date, however, we do not appear to have such plants in cultivation.

H. G. Jones reduced this species, under the name *L. rupestris*, along with *L. longipes*, to synonymy under *L. caulescens* (see *Caldasia* 10: 50, 1970). This nomenclature is erroneous (see *L. longipes*) in light of present opinions and should not be considered further. There is also the possibility that *crispata* and *tereticaulis* may be the same.

Curly-lipped Laelia

Brazil

Laelia crispilabia A. Richard *ex* Warner. 1865. *Select Orch. Plants* 2, t. 6.
  Subgenus: *Parviflorae*
    Section: *Rupestres*

Synonyms

Bletia crispilabia Reichenbachia f. 1863. *Xenia Orch.* 2:61.
Laelia lawrenceana Hort. 1865. *Sel. Orch. Plants* 2, sub. t. 6.
Laelia cinnabarina var. *crispilabia* (A. Rich.) Veitch. 1887. *Man. Orch. Pl.,*
    Laelia, p. 63.

This relatively rare laelia is similar in growth habit to *L. cinnabarina* but has purple or pale magenta flowers. Ghillány describes the plants as growing upon iron ore rock in the Serra de Marinhos in Minas Gerais where they flower in April, May and June. *Laelia flava* grows in the same habitat, only under shrubbery rather than out in the open, according to his reports. The altitude varies from 1000 to 1200 m.

Plants of this species produce two to 4–5 blossoms above the leaves, and the lips characteristically have a long-stalked midlobe, a feature also associated with *L. cinnabarina* flowers. Both a white form and a "blue" *coerulea* form have been described, but otherwise little seems to be known about this species. In Cunha Filho's research (1966) it was considered the congener of *L. caulescens.*

The squat pseudobulbs are 4–5 cm. high and the leathery leaves another 5–6 cm. The plate in *Select Orchidaceous Plants,* depicts the pseudobulbs as long-necked in shape. The dorsal sepal measures 24 × 6 mm., the lateral sepals 20 × 6 mm., the petals 24 × 5 mm. and the lip 15 mm. long and 12 mm. wide. The fine color illustrations of it growing wild in *Native Orchids of Brasil,* however, do not show the long neck. This difference is, perhaps, a consequence of growing the plants with less than optimum light in cultivation. The plants do not show red pigmentation in the foliage, even in strong light.

Fig. 27. *Laelia crispilabia.*

Fig. 28. *Laelia dayana.*
Orchid Album III, plate 132,
1884, as *L. pumila* var. *dayana.*

Day's Laelia

Brazil

Laelia dayana Reichenbach f. 1876. *Gard. Chronicle, n.s. 6: 772*
    Subgenus: *Crispae*
        Section: *Hadrolaelia*

Synonym
Laelia pumila var. *dayana* Burbridge *ex* Dean. 1877. *Floral Mag.* n.s., t. 249.

This laelia was named by Reichenbach after John Day, who sent the famous taxonomist the first specimens from the Day greenhouses at Tottenham. In the description of the species, Reichenbach writes, "An unexpected and lovely plant. Take a *Laelia pumila* and give the lip a very dark purplish border, similar very dark veins covered with dark low lamellae; this is the *Laelia dayana*, named in honor of my excellent correspondent, Mr. Day, who most kindly sent me seven glorious flowers of this new Brazilian plant." (What a fine classical Germanic sentence!) The plants had been sent to England by Boxall, the collector for Hugh Low and Co., mixed in a lot of *L. pumila*.

The single flowers of this species are easily distinguished from those of *pumila* by the 5–7 narrow keels, highest in the center, and the darker color of the flowers, especially the margins of the side lobes and the midlobe of the lip. The prominent veins contrast markedly with the white of the throat. The sepals and petals are described as lilac-mauve, and the lip markings can be a deep velvety purple. Like other hadrolaelias, these have a dwarf habit of growth. Almost invariably the shape of the flowers is poor by judging standards: they don't open widely, the petals droop, the various parts tend to reflex, and the flowers hang down from their stalks. Their attraction comes from the color and form of the lip.

Veitch offered several cultural suggestions for growing these plants in

Fig. 29. *Laelia dayana* var. *coerulea*. Photo by Trudi Marsh.

Fig. 30. *Laelia duveenii*. Photo by Jack Fowlie.

England. They should be in shallow containers suspended near the glass so they receive maximum light and air and a range of temperatures consistent with the seasons: warm during the growing season, and cool, but not below 55°F (13°C), in the dormant period. The limited compost should never be allowed to dry and during growth should be liberally watered.

The plants in nature grow on forest trees in the Organ Mountains of Rio de Janeiro and on north into Minas Gerais at altitudes of 500–800 m. An *alba* variety has been described, and at least one natural hybrid has been noted, *Lc. binoti,* a cross between *L. dayana* and *C. intermedia.*

Duveen's Laelia

Brazil

Laelia duveenii Fowlie. 1988. *Orchid Digest* 52 (4): 180–182.
Subgenus: *Parviflorae*
Section: *Liliputanae*

This is the most recently described of the rupicolous laelia species, and the data had to be inserted into my already "completed" manuscript before it went to the publisher. It is appropriate that it be dedicated to Duveen, as Fowlie states in the description, because of his long interest, field work and writing about this intriguing group of species. At this point, it almost seems never ending as well. The type plants were collected from north of the Serra do Cipó in Diamantina by Papo Firme, though Fowlie suggests it might also be found in the south of the Serra do Cipó.

Two features distinguish it from other species. One is a pleasant fragrance, the other species of rupicolous laelias lacking odors. The other is the observation that it flowers in the Brazilian late fall (May) but November in the Northern Hemisphere, when few other species of this complex taxon are in bloom. Other notable features are a crystalline texture that glistens in good light, rounded and comparatively wide sepals and petals, and a bright rosy lavender-purple color.

It readily falls in the miniature short-stemmed purple-flowered category with pseudobulbs 3.5–5 cm. high, fleshy, red-stained leaves 4–7 cm. long and a flower stalk of approximately equal length. The flower spathe is 1 cm. long, and the stalk bears 2–4 flowers. The dorsal sepal measures 6–8 mm. × 18–20 mm., the lateral sepals slightly smaller. The petals are 6–8 mm. wide and 15–18 mm. long. The lip measures 14–15 × 14–15 mm. with the rounded and flat midlobe 5 mm. across and long. The disc is creamy in color, and the base of the throat is white with a central purple band along the main veins. The ovary and pedicel are 3–4 cm. long.

In the key to the species (Table V), *L. duveenii* falls closest to *L. longipes.* It shares the purple with cream or yellow on the lip pattern with *longipes, ghillanyi, liliputana* and *kettieana.* It has the elongated ovary of *longipes,* but not to quite the same degree, nor do its petals and sepals tend to have the flare pattern that can be found in *longipes.*

This is an attractive new species and will be popular for hybridizing because of its color, fragrance and blooming season.

Fig. 31. *Laelia elegans* 'Wargnyana'. *Lindenia,* plate 535, as *Lc.* Wargnyana.

Elegant Laelia

Brazil

Laelia elegans Reichenbach f. 1855. Otto and Dietrich's *Allg. Gartenzeit.*
23: 242
    Subgenus: *Crispae*
      Section: *Crispae*

Synonyms
Cattleya elegans Morren. 1848. *Ann. Soc. Agr. de Gand.* 4: 93, t. 185.
Laelia brysiana Lemaire. 1856. *Ill. Hort.* 3: 48.
Bletia elegans (Morren) Reichenbach f. 1861. *Walp. Ann. Bot.* 6: 427.
Laelia gigantea Warner. 1862. *Proc. Royal Hort. Soc.* 2: 247.
Laelia turneri Warner. 1864. *Sel. Orch. Pl.* 1, t. 12.
Laelia purpurata brysiana Du Buyss. 1878. *L'Orchid.,* p. 362.
Laelia devoniensis Hort. 1881. *Flor. Mag.,* n.s., sub t. 437.
Laelia pachystele Reichenbach f. 1888. *Gard. Chron.,* 3rd s. 4: 596.
Laeliocattleya elegans (Morren) Rolfe. 1889. *Gard. Chron.* 3rd s. 5: 619.
Laeliocattleya pachystele (Rchb. f.) Rolfe *ex* Williams. 1894. *Orch. Grow. Manual,* 7th ed., p. 459.
Laeliocattleya lindeni Hort. 1894. *Lindenia* 10:33, t. 447.
Laeliocattleya sayana L. Linden. 1894. *Journ. des Orch.* 5:220.
Laeliocattleya schulziana L. Linden. 1895. *Lindenia* 11:21, t. 489.
Catlaelia elegans Hansen. 1895. *Orch. Hybr.,* p. 93.

This species is in reality a natural hybrid between *Laelia purpurata* and *Cattleya leopoldii.* Before its hybrid nature was discovered, however, it was described as several different *Laelia* species and as many different color forms or varieties. There were some 45, at least, according to Cogniaux in *Martius' Flora Brasiliensis* where an extensive list of citations may be found for all of the varieties up to 1902. These plants were very popular, each grower having his favorite types, and many were pictured in the color plate books.

The flowers were generally 12–15 cm. across and amethyst-purple suffused with white, paler in some forms, darker in others. The lips tended to be white inside with dark tips on the lateral lobes and red-purple on the midlobe. Most of the plants identified as *elegans* took after their *purpurata* parent with large-sized flowers, pale color in sepals and petals and the notable pattern of purple color on the lips. Spotted flowers or smaller flowers were called by other names, either *Lc. schilleriana* or *Cattleya intricata*, and were not directly included in the *elegans* concept at all, though they actually represented other forms of the hybrid swarm with greater influence from the *leopoldii* parent (see Withner and Adams, 1960).

Of course, some of the plants in a natural hybrid population would be intermediate between the parents. Others, depending upon the degree of back crossing and/or selfing of the hybrids, show a greater variety of traits as segregation of characteristics occurs. In some locales even a third species, *Cattleya intermedia*, was involved in the hybridity. It is not surprising that some of the plants were bifoliate, others monofoliate in habit of growth. Nor is it surprising, in a population of hybrid origin, that four of the

Fig. 32. *Laelia elegans* 'Prasiata'. *Orchid Album* III, plate 97, 1884.

pollinia were larger in size, the four others smaller. This has often been observed in hybrids between other species of *Cattleya* and *Laelia* and is also true in this case.

This hybrid species is a fine example of introgression (see Chapter 3 in Vol. I of this series) where the gene pools of the two or three parent species are completely intermixed in the hybrid swarm. Some writers prefer the name syngameon, rather than species, for such a hybrid population. In any case, this population was well known and the description of all the various color types gives us ample material to study. I have written elsewhere (*Proc. Third World Orch. Conf. London*, p. 136) of the Santa Catarina Island population of *L. elegans* where this taxon was first discovered. It was later found on the mainland as well.

Laelia elegans flowers in the summer months, from May to September. The plants in nature grow on rocks and cliffs where they are even moistened by sea spray from time to time. They like ample light and good air circulation, as do so many of the laelias, and intermediate temperatures.

Finally, I am sad to note that on a recent trip in Brazil (1989) and after interviews with many orchid nurserymen and hobby growers, I failed to find a single mature plant of this hybrid for sale! One company did have young mericlone plants available of one selected variety, a far cry from the many types popular at the turn of the century. Perhaps it is time to duplicate the hybrid in cultivation with superior selected parents? When that is done, we would call the plants *Lc.* Elegans, using the actually correct generic name for this grex or the hybrid species.

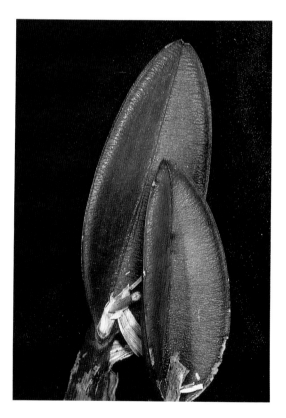

Fig. 33. *Laelia endsfeldzii.*
Rugose leaf surface.
Photo by Trudi Marsh.

Endsfeldz's Laelia

Brazil

Laelia endsfeldzii Pabst. 1975. *Bradea* 2 (10): 51.
Subgenus: *Parviflorae*
Section: *Parviflorae*

This is a little-known species, as so many of the rupicolous laelias seem to be. Recently described, it is found only in a small area near Itutinga in the state of Minas Gerais. It is easily confused with *L. mixta* and *L. blumenscheinii,* and these two are made synonyms of it in Brieger, Maatsch and Senghas' *Die Orchideen.* Careful comparisons among the drawings from the work of Pabst and his collaborators indicates that all three are separate species, as Pabst believed—a concept I follow here as well.

These are long-stemmed laelias, and the flowers, though small, are well separated and open one after the other. This is the habit for several of these *Parviflorae* species, as well as having stalks that are longer than the leaves. The blossoms are pale yellow, starry and with a stalked and ruffled midlobe that curls down and back. When the lip is spread flat, a distinct red area appears at its base on either side of the midline veins.

The furrowed leaves have a definite rugose surface and are red flushed, as are the pseudobulbs. In our specimen the pseudobulbs measure to 10 cm. with the leaf an additional 12 or more cm. The flower stalk reaches 25 cm., the sheath 6 cm. The dorsal sepal is 1.9 cm. long × 5 mm. wide, the lateral sepals only 1.6 cm. long, comparatively short. The petals are 2.0 cm. long × 5 mm. wide, widening from a narrow base and with almost parallel sides. The lip is 10 mm. wide × 14 mm. long.

In Brazil, plants of this species flower in June or July. Hamilton reports three instances of flowering in cultivation, one each in February, May and December, so further experience with these plants is necessary. The species was dedicated to its discoverer, Waldir Endsfeldz, who found it growing in Minas Gerais near Itutinga.

Fig. 34. *Laelia endsfeldzii.* Photo by Trudi Marsh.

Fig. 35. *Laelia esalqueana.* Photo by Trudi Marsh.

Esalqueana Laelia

Brazil

Laelia esalqueana Blumenschein. 1960. *Publ. Cient. Inst. Genetica,*
E.S.A.L.Q. 1:33–44.
> Subgenus: *Parviflorae*
> Section: *Esalqueanae*

The name of this laelia is derived from neither a place nor a person but
is an acronym for *Escola Superior de Agricultura "Luiz de Queiroz"*, an institu-
tion in Piracicaba in the state of São Paulo. It is a small species with flower
stalks that about equal the leaves. The stubby, fat pseudobulbs are about 30
mm. tall; the leaves add about 50 mm. and are thick and heavy with a
strongly concave shape. The plants were found between Gouvêia and
Curvelo in Minas Gerais at an altitude of 1200 m.

The 2–4 flowers are small, about 3 cm. across, and a pale yellow. They
are borne on a stalk about 5 cm. high with a sheath of 12 mm. The dorsal
sepal is 5×17 mm., the lateral sepals 5×14 mm. The petals are 5×15 mm.,
and the lip is 10 mm. long by 9 mm. wide.

The plants flower from November through January in Brazil, from
May through July in the Northern Hemisphere.

Fig. 36. *Laelia fidelensis.* Photo by Trudi Marsh.

Saint Fidel's Laelia

Brazil

Laelia fidelensis Pabst. 1967. *Orquidea* 29 (1):11, t. 6.
Subgenus: *Crispae*
Section: *Crispae*

This laelia species was discovered in 1940 by Dr. Julio Sodre in the São Fidélis Mountains near his village of the same name in the state of Rio de Janeiro. It is located along the Rio Paraiba near Campos. Collected plants were sent to F. C. Hoehne, the Brazilian orchid expert, who declared it a new species, though he never published an official name. There were the usual questions relating to whether it was a natural hybrid or a species. But, after selfed seedlings produced by Rolf Altenburg of Floralia and raised by Orquidário Binot began to flower as a uniform population, it was recognized as a species. In the meantime both Prof. Hoehne and Dr. Sodre had died, and no one knew of the habitat locale where additional plants could be found.

In 1966 a plant in flower collected by a local farmer in São Fidélis was given to Guido Pabst by Lucilio Leite at a Botanical Congress in Rio de Janeiro. Prof. Brieger also agreed it was a species and not a natural hybrid, and anyway, what could the parents have been? So Pabst published the name in 1967. Later a pressed specimen was found in the Herbarium of the

Jardim Botânica do Rio, but no one had previously recognized it as a separate species, nor given it a name. In any case, plants of this species are beginning to appear in American and other collections, most raised from seed.

Compared with other laelias in its cattleya-like group, *L. fidelensis* is small in habit, growing about 30 cm. tall and with 2–3 cm. between growths. The leaves are a definite oblong shape with rounded tips and somewhat narrow, folded bases. There are 1–4 flowers, not more, about 8 cm. across. They are a lavender-pink or rose in color, almost a concolor, but with darker pigmentation along some of the veins and toward the edges of the petals. The petals are somewhat long and pointed at their tips. The trumpet-shaped lip is palely colored in the throat, while the disc is almost white, veined in purple with a rim of darker rose-purple around its edge. The margin is frilled, and the apex of the lip is definitely pointed, the latter a characteristic that occurs in several laelias but in only two or three of their relatives among the cattleyas.

A complete account of this species has been republished by Dr. Fowlie in the July–August, 1977, *Orchid Digest*. Dr. Fowlie has done more than anyone else, through his field work in Brazil and his writings in the *Digest*, to help us straighten out these various *Laelia* species. So many new species, and so many new names for these rupicolous types, have been confusing to most orchid growers. Many do not know of the wealth of material Dr. Fowlie has provided. Nor can they know of the many patient hours over many years spent by Trudi Marsh in photographing many of these species and designing and laying out the formats for the *Digest* articles.

Laelia fidelensis, according to Hamilton's data, flowers from July through August in cultivation; in January and February in Brazil. It is cultivated in baskets or on slabs so that its slightly rambling rhizomes can move about as they grow. The plants like intermediate to cool conditions with good light, like most other laelias.

Deep Yellow Laelia

Brazil

Laelia flava Lindley. 1839. *Bot. Reg.* 25, misc. 88.
   Subgenus: *Parviflorae*
   Section: *Parviflorae*

Synonyms
Laelia caulescens Lindley. 1841. *Bot. Reg.* 27, sub t. 1. (See under that
   species.)
Laelia fulva Lindley *ex* Heynhold. 1846. *Nomencl.* 2:29.
Cattleya flava Beer. 1854. *Prakt. Stud. Fam. Orch.*, p. 210.
Bletia flava (Beer) Reichenbach f. 1861. *Walp. Ann.* 6: 431.
Bletia caulescens (Lindley) Reichenbach f. 1861. *Walp. Ann. Bot.* 6:431
?*Laelia geraensis* Barbosa Rodrigues. 1876. *Rev. Hort.* 45.
Hoffmannseggella flava (Ldl.) Jones. 1970. *Caldasia* 10: 491–495.

This species is one of the most widely distributed laelias in Brazil and has been known in cultivation in England since 1839. It flowered first in the

Fig. 37. *Laelia flava. Orchid Album,* V, plate 226, 1886.

collection of Sir Charles Lemon at Carclew in Cornwall. The plants came
from the Serra da Piedade and the Serra do Frio in Minas Gerais, at eleva-
tions of 800–1000 m. near the town of Lavrinha, as Gardner describes in his
Travels in Brazil, 1836–1841.

Blumenschein, in his published thesis, analyzed the variation in size
and shape of the flowers and vegetative parts of this species from four different localities. He found strong variation in the time of flowering, size of
vegetative structures—pseudobulb length, leaf length, etc.—and in overall flower size, but little variation in flower color or form. The data on
flowering compiled by Hamilton shows two blooming peaks, a major one
from February–April and a minor peak in August–September.

In spite of its wide distribution, Blumenschein showed that the plants
all had the usual diploid chromosome number of 40, forming 20 bivalents
at metaphase I, and interestingly he found no 80-chromosome tetraploid
types as he had in other rock laelia species. Pabst, however, described two
separate populations of this species in his *Orchid Digest* treatise: a
"Southern" variation with smaller flowers and red spots at the base of the
lip, and a "Northern" population lacking the spots and with larger flowers.
He also noted that there are white-flowered variations and also some
plants with golden yellow flowers—however they differed from plain
yellow or deep yellow forms. In this regard the authors of *Native Orchids of
Brasil* distinguish between a sulfur-colored population called "pura" and a
shiny yellow population called "sulina", but there is little further explana-

tion of the differences. The "pura" form grows in savannah areas at 1200 m.; the "sulina" type grows in open sunlight at 700–900 m. The word *sul* in Portuguese means south, so these designations are likely the same as Pabst's "Northern" and "Southern" groups. The "sulina" and "pura" epithets are only horticultural names at present, have not been botanically published to have official status and, in any case, only describe the color variability within this large species population. Without a label to examine, I found in Brazil that no one seemed to know which was which, and at this point I question the validity of such a distinction without more evidence to indicate separate populations.

The stout stems are pseudobulbous at their bases and then long-necked up to a 10 cm. length. Neck length can vary depending upon the amount of light to which the plants have been exposed. The stiff leaves are about 15 cm. long, narrow and pointed, leathery in texture and dark dull green above, somewhat roughened, and with purplish flushes beneath. They are always at an angle to the stem. The flower stalk and the pseudobulbs are also purple-tinted. The medium-sized flowers tend to be clustered at the top of the inflorescence. The lip is frilled on the edges and blunt at the tip, having four thickened veins and verrucosities running its length. The yellow of the flower segments may be faintly veined with red pigment, especially on the petals. The flower stalk rises to 25 cm. with a sheath of 7.3 cm.

Flower measurements on our specimen are: dorsal sepal 8 × 35 mm.; lateral sepals 9 × 29 mm.; petals 11 × 33 mm.; lip 16 mm. wide × 24 mm. long when flattened.

The plants require good drainage at all times, winter dormancy with less water, good light and cool conditions—the conditions that best duplicate the rock habitats of all these small-flowered laelias. The plants of *L. flava* grow on rocks bearing iron ore, apparently not a requirement for potting media in cultivation. Neither are the fires that sometimes sweep the native habitats, charring some of the pseudobulbs and leaves but not completely destroying the plants.

A natural hybrid has been found of *L. flava* × *L. crispata* and described as *L. caetensis* by Pabst in *Bradea* 2 (10): 50, 1975. Being a hybrid between a yellow and a purple-flowered species, the flowers show yellow toward the bases of sepals and petals, more magenta or purple tones toward the tips. Pabst notes that such hybrids between yellow and purple rock laelias have a tendency to produce white flowers with a purple flush on the outside of the flower parts. This tendency in such crosses to produce white flowers has already been noted in two of the *Cattleya* hybrids described in Vol. I of this series: *C. hardyana* and *C. guatemalensis*. This characteristic has a connection with the inheritance patterns of carotenoid pigments, but these patterns are not understood at present.

Nor is another fascinating point involving color inheritance explained. An occasional plant of this species, perhaps one in several thousand, has orange instead of yellow flower color, but otherwise is like a typical plant of *L. flava*. They have come to be known as *L. flava* var. *aurantiaca*, a horticultural epithet that has been in use since the first such plant was displayed in 1895 by The Right Honorable Lord Rothschild of Tring Park and his grower, a Mr. E. Hill. It is described in the *Gardeners' Chronicle*

Fig. 38. *Laelia flava* var. *aurantiaca.*

17, 3rd series (433):468 as differing from the type by having "glowing pure orange color". The plant received an Award of Merit. Write-ups of the same display were also published in the *Orchid Review* (Jan., 1895, p. 159) and in the *Journal des Orchidées* (May, 1895, p. 61), but the flowers were never pictured in these original accounts.

The flowers are illustrated on p. 47 of the first edition of the A.O.S. *Handbook on Orchid Culture* (1971) and on the frontispiece of the Brazilian July–August 1954 *Orquidea;* the only published pictures that I could find. With my old slide of that plant, taken so long ago in Brooklyn, sent to the Botanic Garden as part of an orchid shipment from Orquidário Binot, I can add another to the record. I am assured, incidentally, by the Verboonens at Binot that this color phase does not represent a separate species and is only a very occasional variant in the ordinarily yellow, wild population. Needless to say, more plants should be raised by selfing or by sib crossing two such wild plants to see if the color comes through. It should be a good variety for breeding high color once it becomes available. This would be in contrast to the ordinary yellow forms of this species, often used in hybrids, but with disappointing results as the yellow color is not ordinarily a dominant trait in the progeny.

Fig. 39. *Laelia furfuracea.* A rare white form.

Scurfy Laelia

México

Laelia furfuracea Lindley. 1839. *Bot. Reg.* 25, t. 26.
Subgenus: *Laelia*
Section: *Podolaelia*

Synonyms
Cattleya furfuracea (Lindley) Beer. 1854. *Prakt. Stud. Fam. Orch.*, p. 210.
Bletia furfuracea (Lindley) Reichenbach f. 1861. *Walp. Ann. Bot.* 6:428.

This species gets its name from the tiny, dark brown or black scales that cover the ovary and some of the flower stalk resulting from the minute glands located in those parts. Their function is not known. There are as many as three flowers on one inflorescence, seldom more, while 1–2 seem most common. They are an overall rose-purple with darker purple on the midlobe of the lip.

This species and *L. speciosa* have short flower stalks compared to other Méxican-Central American taxa of this genus. This quality, plus the mealy scales and the short, ridged pseudobulbs, make the species easy to recognize. It grows in the state of Oaxaca and is often picked by the hundreds for sale at Christmas time. It is known by the local terms of *monjita* (Little Nun) and *lirio*, a common Latin American term for lily, also used for certain cattleyas in South America. It occurs at high altitudes in the mountains, from 2500–3000 m., usually on the rough bark of scrubby oaks. The flowers are picked by breaking off the lead pseudobulb with its attached spike so that the flowers will last. This treatment gives most orchid growers a twinge when they see such bouquets, but conservationists claim that it promotes more growths from the backbulbs and ultimately results in greater plant production. The locals have, of course, been doing it for years.

Veitch notes that this species was first discovered by Count Karwinsky about 1832 and was introduced into England in 1838 in the collection of Barker in Birmingham. The plants are small, with pear-shaped pseudobulbs about 3–5 cm. tall bearing a single, pointed, leathery, stiff leaf that varies from about 5 cm. to somewhat more than 10–12 cm. in length. There are two keels or ridges in the throats of the flowers, and the petals tend toward a diamond-shape, wide relative to their length. The tip of the lip is reflexed and the column colored a rose-pink. It grows in habitats similar to those of *L. autumnalis* but lacks the white lateral lobes on the lip and the greater size of plant and length of flower stalk typical of that species.

A white form of this species is known, but otherwise there is little variation in flower color to prompt assigning varietal recognition. It has not been common in collections which probably accounts for the absence of named clones. The plant has had the reputation of being difficult to grow, dying out after two or three years. Greater attention to providing cool conditions, a real dormancy with little or no water, but good humidity, mounting on cork or slabs, and hanging the plants in good light year around should resolve those problems. The natural hybrid with *L. speciosa* is *L. venusta* and with *L. albida* is *L. leucoptera*. A presumed natural hybrid, called *L. ashworthii* in California, may be related to the latter.

Gardner's Laelia

Brazil

Laelia gardneri Pabst. 1975. *Bradea* 2 (6): 21–24.
  Subgenus: *Parviflorae*
    Section: *Rupestres*

Synonym
Laelia longipes sensu Cogniaux, *non* Rchb. f. *Martius' Flora Brasiliensis*
  3(5):277, pl. 65

Section *Rupestres* is marked by plants producing tall flower stalks, higher than the leaves, and lavender or purple flowers. This species fits that bill and is named after its original collector in Brazil, Gardner, who collected there 1836–1841. His type specimen was first misidentified by Reichenbach f. as *L. longipes*, actually a short flower-stalked species named for its elongated pedicel and ovary. Years later, recognized for what it really was by Pabst, the species was then named properly.

The flowers have a pale lavender-purple blush while the crisped lip,

Fig. 40. *Laelia gardneri.* Photo by Trudi Marsh.

with three main ridges running its length, is a lemony yellow with white in the throat. It has broad sepals and the lip is rounded at its apex, much frilled and tightly recurved in almost a full circle. This combination of features along with its tall flower stalk make for a unique species in the purple-flowered rock laelia complex, especially the all-yellow lip. The other species in *Parviflorae* with yellow lips are *L. lucasiana* and *L. reginae* in the *Liliputanae.*

The plants are small, about 10 cm. high, though the flower stalk can reach 30 cm. with a sheath of 1.5 cm. The flower parts on one specimen measure as follows: dorsal sepal 6 × 16 mm.; the lateral sepals 7 × 13 mm.; petals 4.5 × 17 mm.; lip about 8 mm. wide × 12 mm. long—impossible to flatten out completely. It is grown like other rock laelia species and comes from Mosteiro da Caraca in Minas Gerais. The plate of *L. longipes* in *Martius' Flora Brasiliensis* 3(5):plate 65 is a picture of this species with the wrong name, as mentioned above.

Ghillány's Laelia

Brazil

Laelia ghillanyi Pabst. 1973. *Bradea* 1 (31): 332.
    Subgenus: *Parviflorae*
       Section: *Liliputanae*

The Baron Ghillány is an avid collector of and writer about Brazilian orchid species who also sells orchids commercially. It is not surprising that he has discovered more than one of the endemic rock laelias, in this case between the Serra do Cipó and Conceição do Mato Dentro in Minas Gerais, where the plants grow on volcanic rock at 1500–1600 m. They also may be found in sandy soil among bromeliads, as described by Odebrecht (1988). In Brazil the plants flower September–November; in cultivation in the Northern Hemisphere May–July.

The flowers of this species are a magenta purple with very pale color or white in the throat, the paleness spreading out on the disc. The plants produce 2–3 flowers on a short stalk that scarcely exceeds the leaves. A unique feature of the flowers is the column, being more distinctly winged than other species, so that from the side it appears about twice as wide at the base as at the tip, instead of a uniform width from top to bottom.

The stubby pseudobulbs are 5–7 cm. high and about 2.5 cm. in diameter at the base. The leaves are 10–15 cm. long, and are so succulent and stiff as to be nearly terete. The plants are usually flushed with maroon, especially on the pseudobulbs and the edges of the leaf. The flower stalk reaches 10 cm. with a sheath of 1.5 cm. The dorsal sepal is 7 × 18 mm. and the lateral sepals are somewhat smaller. The petals measure 9 × 18 mm. The lip is wider than long, 14.5 mm. × 12 mm.

A white form of this species has been described, as well as one natural hybrid. The latter is *L. cipoensis*, formally described by Pabst in *Bradea* 2(4): 14, with the other parent being *L. crispata*. The hybrid has purple flowers, as would be expected, the tall flower stalk of the *crispata*, and the wide column base from the *ghillanyi*. It flowers in November in Brazil. An *alba* form of the hybrid has also been described.

Fig. 41. *Laelia ghillanyi.*

Fig. 42. *Laelia gloedeniana.* Photo by Jorge Verboonen.

Gloeden's Laelia

Brazil

Laelia gloedeniana Hoehne. 1933. *Bol. Agricola de São Paulo* 34: 624.
Subgenus: *Parviflorae*
Section: *Parviflorae*

Synonym
Laelia macrobulbosa Pabst. 1973. *Bradea* 1 (31): 335.

Only a few of the *Parviflorae* laelias are found in the mountains of the state of Espírito Santo, this species and two others: *blumenscheinii* and *mixta*. Other species are found further inland, mostly in the mountains of Minas Gerais that parallel the coastal Espírito Santo locations. The plants of this species are rare, according to Pabst, and occur in the Pedra de Severina at about 1600 m. where they grow with a bromeliad, *Pitcairnia decidua*. The pale yellow flowers with red veining and red on the base of the lip presumably make it easily distinguishable. I would note here, however, that *L. endsfeldzii* also shows the same characteristic red at the base of the lip, and I have also seen it in flowers of *L. flava*. This red is also a characteristic of *L. macrobulbosa* flowers, a species best reduced now to synonymy under *gloedeniana*.

The flowers are relatively large, about 5–6 cm. across, on a tall stalk that extends above the leaf. The pseudobulbs measure 20–25 cm. high and the leaves 30–50 cm. long. Up to 10 flowers may be produced, opening in succession. The individual flowers bear a superficial similarity to those of *L.*

flava, but the shape and length of the midlobe of the lip distinguish it properly. Flower parts measure 6 mm. × 25 mm. for dorsal sepal, 5 mm. × 24 mm. for petals, 6 mm. × 23 mm. for lateral sepals and lip 12 mm. wide and 18 mm. long. It flowers from March–May in Brazil, February–April in the Northern Hemisphere.

The plants of *L. macrobulbosa* deserve special mention as their robust pseudobulbs, unusually thick, measured 4.5–5 cm. through at the base and were 20 cm. high. The leathery, thick, oblong leaves added another 20 cm. The flowers, though slightly smaller than typical *gloedeniana* flowers, were similar in color and markings, but the flower stalk was short, first placing the species in the section *Esalqueanae* instead of with the section *Parviflorae* where it belonged. The problem was one of light and water affecting growth—not the taxonomic nomenclature!

All these rock laelias, indeed even most plants, have their growth habits influenced strongly by growing conditions—height of the plant, area and length of the leaves, the texture and substance of the leaves, the size of flowers and, especially for orchids, the shape and size of pseudo-bulbous stems. This is particularly noticeable when collected plants from the wild are brought into cultivation. This situation involved plants from two different localities, and although they were the same species they appeared sufficiently distinct to warrant two names. One population must have grown in a drier, brighter habitat than the other, thus producing the macro-pseudobulbs and short flower stalks. I think that the presence of short velvety hairs inside the lip, mentioned by Pabst, can also be accounted for in this fashion. The type of *L. macrobulbosa* was collected near Indaia in Espírito Santo by Ghillány and first flowered in cultivation in April, 1973. Gloeden was an orchid hunter and dealer in plants.

Gould's Laelia

México

Laelia gouldiana Reichenbach f. 1888. *Gard. Chron.*, 3rd s., 3:41.
    Subgenus: *Laelia*
        Section: *Podolaelia*

No description of this species can be found in several of the early horticultural books, such as Veitch's *Manual*, and there has been a question of whether it is a form of or the same as *L. autumnalis*. Some authorities, such as Williams in *Orchidaceae of México*, list it as a synonym under that species. Others have raised the question of whether it is extinct in the wild, living now only in cultivation where it has been naturalized around ranches and homes, brought in from the wild in years past. My colleagues in México, however, inform me that it is alive and well, though not common, in the wild in the state of Hidalgo, where it grows in the cool, dry mountains.

Other orchidists have opined that *L. gouldiana* is a single clone, all present plants in cultivation being divisions of one original plant. It is famous for showing very little variation, true, but that is hardly the case

Fig. 43. *Laelia gouldiana.* Photo by Trudi Marsh.

either. And, of course, there is the natural hybrid idea, a cross between *L. anceps* and *L. autumnalis,* first proposed by Reichenbach. The hybrid was later produced in cultivation by Sir George Holford and called *L. Alexanderae.* Since it was different from this species, the idea of the species being a natural hybrid was abandoned. It is close to *autumnalis,* but the flowers are much brighter in color, the petals are broader and the lip is slightly different. Rolfe, in the *Orchid Review,* also notes that it has longer bracts.

The first plants of this species to be cultivated found their way into American collections through Siebrecht and Wadley of New York, a change from the usual English or European introduction for most of the species, and were named after New York financier Jay Gould. I have not been able to track down any other details about its introduction into cultivation. It was popular in England, where it was described in the *Orchid Album,* plate 371, and Sir Trevor Lawrence was recognized for his plant that had 10 spikes and more than 40 flowers. Since it flowers in December and January, it was all the more popular.

The clustered pseudobulbs are 8–12 cm. high, smooth when young, but becoming corrugated or ridged with age. There are two leaves, pointed, elongated and leathery, 15 cm. or more in length, deep green often flushed with red in bright light. The 6–10 cm. flowers are borne on a scape about 30 cm. long, and 2 to 4–5 are produced.

The flowers are a bright rose to red-purple, darker and brighter toward the tips of the petals. The lateral lobes of the lip are also a rosy purple, and the apex of the lip is a deeper red-purple. The three keeled veins coming from the throat are a bright yellow, the contrast making them easily seen.

This species has been used only a few times in hybridization, mostly in the last few years. One interesting cross registered by Armacost and Royston is between *L. anceps* and this species. Significantly, it is called *L. Lookalike*. Since there is an apparent uniformity among clones, most of the recognition of this species by the A.O.S. is in the form of cultural certificates.

Graceful Laelia

Brazil

Laelia gracilis Pabst. 1979. *Bradea* 2: 314.
Subgenus: *Parviflorae*
Section: *Parviflorae*

The original description is the source of most information about this laelia, the name being derived from the fact that the unusually tall flower stalk curves gracefully under the weight of the flowers. The deep reddish purple plants with scapes are up to 45 cm. tall, the scape 35 cm. long itself. Coming from the rocky areas of the Serra do Cipó in Minas Gerais, they flower in August and September in Brazil, but are not mentioned among Hamilton's data covering cultivation.

The 5–7 small flowers are a pale yellow. The dorsal sepal measures 5 × 16 mm., the lateral sepals 5 × 13 mm. The petals are a little wider, to measure 5.5–6 × 16 mm. The lip undulations are pronounced with the flattened lip measuring 9–10 mm. wide and 13–14 mm. long. It has a short stalk, in the fashion of the lip midlobe of *L. cinnabarina*. Four main veins may be noted on the disc. Little of this species is known in cultivation at present.

Fig. 44. *Laelia gracilis*. Photo by Trudi Marsh.

Fig. 45. *Laelia grandis.*

Grand Laelia

Brazil

Laelia grandis Lindley. 1850. *Paxton's Flower Garden* 1:60
Subgenus: *Crispae*
Section: *Crispae*

Synonym
Bletia grandis (Lindley) Reichenbach f. 1861. *Walp. Ann. Bot.* 6: 424.

In contrast with most other Brazilian laelias, if not almost all laelias, the plants of this species are warm growers. They come from Bahia around the bay of Todos os Santos, also northernmost Espírito Santo. The first plants were sent by Pinel to Morel in Paris in 1849, and it was exhibited in London the following year. Then, in 1864 more plants were sent to Low and Co. by their collector in Bahia. Lindley apparently named it in reference to its large pseudobulbs and leaves.

The plants are typically cattleya-like, characteristic of this section of the *Laelia* genus. They produce 2–5 flowers as much as 12–14 cm. across. The sepals and petals are wavy and twisted or are reflexed along the midribs, which makes them unpopular as breeding stock, but their nankeen yellow color compensates for the shape. This kind of yellow usually has a bronzy cast similar to that of old raw silk. The tube of the lip is generally white, but in some clones it is rose-stained on the midlobe. In the throat the white is veined with rose-purple, and the veining is prominently extended toward the apex of the lip, there being a darker, almost solidly colored region on each side of the bell. The column has a green color and is speckled with purple, especially on the bottom.

Plants flower May–July in our cultivation. Since they have been difficult to obtain from the wild for some time, Orquidário Binot, for one, has been raising them from seed to supply the trade. Even so, they are not often seen in collections. At one time *L. tenebrosa* was considered a variety of this species, but it is now recognized as a separate entity although there are certain similarities. The species is also closely related to *L. xanthina*, and these three species, *grandis*, *xanthina* and *tenebrosa*, are the exception to the cool rule for growing laelias.

A natural hybrid between *L. grandis* and *C. warneri* is named *Lc. albanensis*, and there is also a hybrid between this species and *C. amethystoglossa* that has been duplicated in cultivation, *Lc.* Pittiana. The name, *Lc. pittiana*, has also been applied in the literature to a natural hybrid between *L. tenebrosa* × *C. leopoldii*. Few named clones of *grandis* seem to turn up in the old records, probably reflecting its twisty shape, but it has been used over the years to produce a number of hybrids in cultivation. The cultivar 'Platysepala' is significantly named because of its flat sepals, while cultivar 'Leucoglossa' has almost no veining on the lip.

Hernani Urpía of Salvador, Bahia, has written one of the few first-hand accounts of the habitat of this species growing high on 80-ft.-tall *jequitiba* trees in full sun. The plants had to be spotted from the ground with binoculars. Also found in the same region were *C. warneri*, *C. amethystoglossa* and *C. leopoldii*, as well as other types of orchids. This distribution can certainly account for the natural hybrids mentioned above. On the other hand, *L. tenebrosa* and *L. xanthina*, though closely related, could not be found in the region. Urpía mentions finding massive clumps of this laelia, one specimen having 28 flowers on four growths, 4–6 flowers per growth. The flowers are not fragrant. In its habitat it flowers in October.

Sickle-leaf Laelia

Brazil

Laelia harpophylla Reichenbach f. 1873. *Gard. Chron.*, p. 542.
  Subgenus: *Parviflorae*
  Section: *Harpophyllae*

Synonyms
Laelia geraensis Barb. Rodr. 1876. *Revista de Hort.*, p. 45.
Bletia harpophylla (Rchb. f.) Reichenbach f. 1888. *Reichenbachia*, I, 89.
Hoffmannseggella harpophylla (Rchb. f.) Jones. 1970. *Caldasia* 10:491–495.

The epiphytic nature of the species in the *Harpophyllae* section is always emphasized and is one of the major distinctions of the taxon, in contrast to the rock habitats of the other species that make up the subgenus *Parviflorae*. The plants of this species flowered in cultivation in 1867 in the collections of Rucker and Day. It has remained popular because of its brightly colored blossoms, its ease of culture and its ability to produce specimen plants. The flower stalks are shorter than the leaves. The leaves are narrow, pointed and curved, giving rise to the Greek *harpe* designation meaning sickle- or sword-shaped.

The plant habit is easy to recognize as the clustered stems are not thickened, are about as thick as pencils, and are cylindrical from top to base.

They may be as much as 45 cm. tall with the leaf another 25 cm. in fully grown examples. The 5–8 or more flowers are somewhat crowded together at the top of the flower stalk and are an intense, bright orange. Petals measure 35–40 mm. long, and the lip is 14–17 mm. across the lateral lobes and 25–30 mm. long. The lip is creamy colored on the midlobe that is long, strap-like, distinctly narrow, crisped on the edges and strongly curled back at the apex. The veining is orange on the creamy background. Plants with flowers that appear similar, but have an oval-shaped midlobe on the lip, and a paler more yellow color, are likely *L. kautskyana*; and *L. brevicaulis*, also in this section, has yellow flowers.

Laelia harpophylla is a cool, but not cold, grower and likes a little more water than the rupicolous types of laelia. Nor does it require a dormant period or such intense light. It grows from 500–900 m. in Espírito Santo and in Minas Gerais, blooming July–September in Brazil, peaking in February–March when grown in northern countries.

Pabst has described a natural hybrid, *L. harpophylla* × *L. kautskyana*, that he calls *L.* × *gerhardt-santosi*. The midlobe of the lip is intermediate between the two parents. In fact, according to the Verboonens at Orquidário Binot, there can be such variation in lip width that it is difficult to tell where the hybrid variation stops and the parental variation begins. Once again we may be dealing with the effects of introgression between two species. Several cultivated hybrids have been made with *harpophylla*, whose color comes through in crosses, a dominance that does not always occur when other laelia species are used as parents.

Fig. 46. *Laelia harpophylla.* Photo by Trudi Marsh.

Fig. 47. *Laelia harpophylla.* Lip detail. Photo by Trudi Marsh.

Hispid Laelia

Brazil

Laelia hispidula Pabst and Mello. 1978. *Bradea* 2(33): 227–231.
Subgenus: *Parviflorae*
Section: *Rupestres*

This laelia is more of a puzzle than anything else, but it is illustrated in at least two photos in *Native Orchids of Brasil.* Fowlie indicates that there is no actual type specimen for the species, but rather a drawing and a photograph of a plant in cultivation, these constituting a *lectotype,* in Pabst's Herbarium. Before he died Pabst was of the opinion that this taxon might be a natural hybrid of *L. crispata* × *L. angereri* (though neither of these is hispid), but as of now it is still considered a separate species. Less is known about this laelia than most of the others.

The most unique feature of the flowers is the hispid nature of the base of the lip inside the throat. This stiff hairiness (which could be an artifact from the drying of the flowers for the herbarium) is also known in one of the yellow species, *L. gloedeniana* (*L. macrobulbosa*) that comes from Espírito Santo farther north. *Laelia hispidula* comes from the Serra da Tamamboia at 1200 m. in Minas Gerais, 60 km. north of Diamantina. Obviously this area should be revisited.

The flowers are a salmon color with purple flushes, as might be expected from a hybrid between yellow- and lavender-flowered taxa, but that may just be the natural color. The lip is pale at the base and in the throat, flushed with color on the outside, and the pointed apical portion is edged with a dark purple with the white or pale salmon on the disc. The stalks produce 8–9 flowers rather crowded together toward their tips. The scapes measure 21.5 cm. tall with 19 cm. high robust pseudobulbs and leaves measuring 19 cm. long.

If or when other specimens become available, the question of hybrid vs. species will have to be settled; it can't be done now with the information at hand. In the type specimen the dorsal sepal is 6 × 19 mm., lateral

Fig. 48. *Laelia hispidula.*
Type illustration from
Pabst Herbarium records
by Dr. Jack Fowlie.

sepals 6.5 × 19 mm., petals 5 × 20 mm. and lip flattened 14 mm. long and 12 mm. across. The unique features are, of course, the hispid quality of the lip, the color, and the pointed apex of the midlobe.

Itambe Laelia

Brazil

Laelia itambana Pabst. 1973. *Bradea* 1(31): 333.
Subgenus: *Parviflorae*
Section: *Esalqueanae*

This species has yellow flowers, and the stalk is about the height of the leaf. There are only two other species with these general characteristics, *L. bradei and L. esalqueana*. The flowers are a starry shape, a concolor overall, and lateral lobes when flattened almost as long as the midlobe and over-lapping it. A particularly distinguishing feature of the flower is the long pedicel and ovary, 4 cm., equalling the length in *L. longipes* flowers that are so named because of this feature. But they, of course, have rosy purple, not yellow, flowers.

Two flowers are produced per stalk in December–January in Brazil. The pseudobulbs are 3–5 cm. high and the leaves, red-flushed on the back, another 7–8 cm. and at an angle. The flower stalk is about 20–25 cm., and the sheath is 1.5 cm. The flowers are comparatively large for the size of the plant, the dorsal sepal 6 × 20 mm. in one specimen, 10 × 25 mm. in the type. The lateral sepals range 6 × 18 mm. to 12 × 20 mm., the petals 6 × 20 mm. to 12 × 23 mm. The flattened lip in our specimen measures 11 mm. long × 10 mm. wide; in the type it is 15 mm. in both directions.

Pabst says in his description that the flowers are similar to those of *L. briegeri*, but have two smooth lamellae instead of four roughened keels. The plants were found on the summit of the Pico do Itambe at 2000–2300 m. in Minas Gerais and were named after the locale. They were collected by W. Anderson, M. Stieber and J. Kirkbride in February, 1972. Hamilton's book gives three reports of June flowering in the Northern Hemisphere.

Fig. 49. *Laelia itambana* 'Riopelle' CHM/AOS. Photo by Hugh Henry.

Fig. 50. *Laelia jongheana* 'Vivian' HCC/AOS. Photo by Trudi Marsh.

Jonghe's Laelia

Brazil

Laelia jongheana Reichenbach f. 1872. *Flora* 55:158
Subgenus: *Crispae*
Section: *Hadrolaelia*

Synonym
Bletia jongheana Reichenbach f. 1872. *Flora* 55: 158.

The short plants with one or two proportionately large flowers of bright amethyst purple color make this a striking laelia. This is especially true since it is rare, only recently having become more common in collections after seedlings raised in cultivation became available through Orquidário Binot and other dealers. The flowers measure 10–13 cm. across, have seven high orange keels in the throat which is pale, almost white, as is the disc. The margin of the lip is finely crisped and frilled.

The pseudobulbs are short and stubby, almost like those on an *Encyclia* when the plants are grown in bright light, but they lengthen and thin down under more usual conditions of cultivation. The leaves are stiff and thick, almost succulent-like. As one might guess, the plants like a good dormancy with cool, bright surroundings. It is difficult to keep plants thriving in the greenhouse unless dormancy is made a priority, otherwise the grower may be rewarded by the rotting of the plants. They do best when mounted on slabs of cork or firm pieces of tree fern that will last

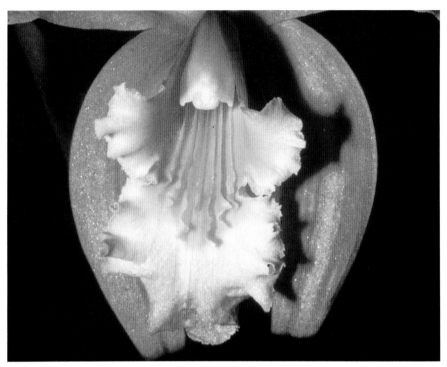

Fig. 51. *Laelia jongheana.* Detail of lip with keels typical of *Hadrolaelia.* Photo by Trudi Marsh.

several years. The plants are quite deliberate in the way they grow and flower, and little can be done to rush them along. Seedlings seem especially difficult for many collections. A well grown plant of this species is a good challenge for one's orchid growing abilities, but the flowers make the effort worth it. The 1987 Butterworth Prize for outstanding culture went to a plant of this species grown by Don Anderson of East Northport, N. Y. The plant, 'Adam York', received a CCM/AOS of 90 points for its beautiful display of 15 flowers.

Laelia jongheana flowers in cultivation from February–April. Originally plants came from around Itabira near Belo Horizonte, in Minas Gerais, but they were over-collected and are now gone. More recently a new locale near Diamantina in the Serra do Espinhaço was discovered. An *alba* form, still with the orangey keels, is known. Many hybrids were produced from this species in the past, but most are unknown today. There is a resurgence of interest now as hobbyists have learned to grow it, so perhaps other hybrids will be available soon, given the modern preference for small plants with large, bright flowers.

The original plants of this species were discovered in Brazil by Libon about 1854, and sent to de Jonghe in Brussels. It was named for de Jonghe at the request of Libon, who unfortunately died soon after while still in Brazil. Nothing more was known of the species until 1872 when it appeared in French collections again and simultaneously was also found in the Veitch Nursery, their plant serving for the illustration published in the *Botanical Magazine,* t. 6038, 1873.

Kautsky's Laelia

Brazil

Laelia kautskyana Pabst *emend.* 1974. *Bradea* 1 (47): 472.
  Subgenus: *Parviflorae*
  Section: *Harpophyllae*

Synonym
Laelia harpophylla var. *dulcotensis* Hort. 1900. *Orchid Review* 8: 122–123.

The first thing to say about this laelia is that the orchidist should not confuse it with *L. kautskyi* as was done in 1969 by Pabst and Dungs for a plant that was later properly named *L. espirito-santensis*. The latter was a natural hybrid between *L. pumila* and *L. xanthina*. The correct name here is *L. kautskyana*; it also comes from Espírito Santo, where it may be found growing with plants of *L. harpophylla*. In fact, it has a vegetative habit just like *L. harpophylla* and for many years was not distinguished from it, nor from their natural hybrid. Roberto Kautsky pointed out this difference, and Pabst named the species after him. Also mixed into this confusion was the so-called "yellow *harpophylla*" that is now more properly called *L. brevicaulis* (please see), thus covering all of the species in the section *Harpophyllae* with their pencil-thin pseudobulbs.

This epiphytic species grows at about 600 m. and flowers in July–August in Brazil, January–February in the Northern Hemisphere. It produces as many as 10 flowers on a stalk. They open an off-yellow color and mature as a clear orange and may be quickly distinguished from

Fig. 52. *Laelia kautskyana.* Photo by Ron Parsons.

harpophylla by differences in the midlobe of the lip. Whereas the midlobe of *harpophylla* is long and uniformly narrow, the midlobe of this species is rounded or somewhat oval in shape. The lip of their natural hybrid, *L. gerhard-santosi*, is intermediate in shape, its most distinguishing feature compared to the appearance of the parents. This hybrid was named after Arthur Carlos Gerhard Santos, the Governor of Espírito Santo, but it may be difficult to distinguish from its *kautskyana* parent.

The *kautskyana* midlobe is pale in color, almost creamy, has somewhat ruffled edges and curls back at the tip as do most of these laelias in the *Parviflorae*, but it is not narrow and strap-like. The petals are shorter for their width, 8×28 mm., than those of *harpophylla* which are 4×30 mm., and the lip is 14 mm. wide (across the lateral lobes) $\times 21$ mm. long. The plants flower about a month later than those of *harpophylla*.

Kettie's Laelia

Brazil

Laelia kettieana Pabst. 1975. *Bradea* 2 (22): 153.
Subgenus: *Parviflorae*
Section: *Liliputanae*

This is a truly miniature species, similar in size to *L. reginae*, and although some authors place it with the *Rupestres* section, it seems to me to fit better with the *Liliputanae* taxon. The flower stalk is not 2–4 times the length of the leaf, typical of the *Rupestres* alliance, only about twice or less, which better places it with the other "micro-miniatures".

The flowers are a rosy lavender color with distinct yellow on the disc of the midlobe. The tip of the lip is margined in a darker reddish purple or magenta, and the tips of the lateral lobes are pinkish. Tips of the sepals and petals are pointed, and the flowers are about 2 cm. in diameter. In our specimen the dorsal sepal measures 3.5×12 mm., the lateral sepals 3.5×10 mm., the petals 4×12 mm. The lip when flat measures 9 mm. long $\times 8$ mm. wide. In the type description the flowers are larger, dorsal sepal 6×22 mm., lateral sepals 5.5×16 mm., petals 5.5×18 and the lip is 13 mm. long $\times 11$ mm. wide. The differences between flowers grown in cultivation and in the wild thus become apparent in this difficult group where culture is critical, especially the amount of light, when shape and measurements are involved.

The plants were first collected in the Serra da Moeda near Caete in Minas Gerais by Kettie Waras, wife of Eddie Waras, who is an enthusiastic Brazilian collector and grower. The plants were also found once in the Serra da Caraça. The latter flowered from October–December. This translates, by Hamilton's data, to May flowering in this country. One or two flowers are produced per stalk.

Fig. 53. *Laelia kettieana.*

Fig. 54. *Laelia liliputana.*

Lilliput Laelia

Brazil

Laelia liliputana Pabst. 1973. *Bradea* 1 (31): 327–336, t. IIIA.
Subgenus: *Parviflorae*
Section: *Liliputanae*

The plants of this "micro-miniature" species are certainly the smallest of the purple-flowered species and vie for the smallest-in-the-genus category with *L. bradei* in the yellow-flowered division. Even in full flower with its single bloom, it is only 6 cm. high, and may only measure 5 cm. It was collected by the Baron Anton Ghillány in the Serra do Ouro Branco in Minas Gerais.

The little plants have stiff, upright, dark green leaves with red flushes, plump pseudobulbs to 15 mm. and the leaf 10–15 mm. on top. The scape is about 1 cm. long with a sheath equally long, and then the solitary flower, an intense, rosy color. The dorsal sepal is 4 × 14 mm., lateral sepals 4 × 12.5 mm., petals 3.5 × 15 mm. The lip is nearly round, the lateral lobes extending almost as far as the midlobe, 7–8 mm. in both length and width. There are four yellow, main veins on the disc.

Lobed Laelia

Brazil

Laelia lobata (Lindley) Veitch. 1887. *Man. Orch. Pl.* II, p. 74
Subgenus: *Crispae*
Section: *Crispae*

Synonyms
Cattleya lobata Lindley. 1848. *Gard. Chron., p. 403.*
Laelia boothiana Reichenbach f. 1853. *Algem. Gartenz.* 23:322.
Laelia grandis var. *purpurea* Reichenbach f. 1854. *Bonplandia* II, p. 89.
Laelia virens Hort. (*non*-Lindley) *ex* Reichenbach f. 1858. *Xenia Orch.* I, p. 218.
Bletia lobata (Lindley) Reichenbach f. 1861. *Walp. Ann. Bot.* 6: 424.
Bletia boothiana (Rchb. f.) Reichenbach f. 1862. *Xenia Orch.* II, p. 51.
Laelia rivieri Carriere. 1874. *Rev. Hort.,* p. 331.

For what began as a little-known laelia, this species has garnered more than its share of synonyms. It was first named a *Cattleya* by Lindley after it flowered in Loddiges' Nursery in 1847. Later Reichenbach named it after Lorenz Booth from Flotbeck, in whose collection it flowered in Germany, but little was known of its origins other than the area of southern Brazil. Veitch is the first to have properly placed it with the laelias because of its eight pollinia, and by then it was known from only one place on the coast of Rio de Janeiro where it grows high on rocks fully exposed to sun, wind and spray from the ocean. Some of the plants are still there in inaccessible places. It distinctly prefers rock faces where it grows among bromeliads and other rock inhabitants. Lindley named the plant *lobata* because of a great amount of "lobing" of the petals and lip which is really just a lot of frilling and wavy edging, not actual indentations or lobes.

Fig. 55. *Laelia lobata.* Photo by Trudi Marsh.

The plant in Booth's collection had grown there for several years and was known as "the Cattleya That Never Flowers". It still has the reputation of being a "shy bloomer", but the plants really seem to be victims of too careful care, especially in the matter of repotting. It has been observed several times and also remarked upon that once the plants reach the edge of the pot they begin to bloom. The normal procedure of repotting before the plant is over the edge is what actually keeps it from flowering! So, growers should let it grow over the edge, and resist the temptation to repot for two or three more cycles in order to have still more blooms. The severe habitat in which it normally grows is best duplicated by this procedure, and unless the plants are stressed with sun and heat with bare roots in the air, they will not be prompted to flower. Obviously they do best in baskets or mounted so that these procedures can be followed.

The plants grow to about 60–70 cm. height, and the flower stalks produce up to five flowers. The flowers are a uniform purple-tinged violet, and with rich red-purple veins, particularly three central ones, in the throat and out over the midlobe of the lip with many branchings and a pansy-violet background. The throat itself is white or with a lemony tint. The sepals measure 2 × 7.5 cm., and the petals are 4.5 × 7.3 cm. The column is white at the base, tinted violet-rose at the tip, and the anther cap is nearly black.

Urpía's firsthand observations are still helpful (A.O.S.B. 23 (7):463, 1954); he tells of darker and clearer colored clones, and also a rare white form that is still in some collections today. It is difficult, however, to find well-shaped flowers without the excessive frilling and reflexing so characteristic of the Brazilian cattleya-like laelias.

This species has been little used in hybridization, likely because it is seldom seen in flower. Its tolerance of stress and reasonably good color should make it a desirable parent in hybrids. In addition, it has a distinct and sweet fragrance. The white form is particularly fine; out of flower the plants look very much like *L. crispa* with the same leaf and bulb characteristics. Urpía remarks that its distribution extends on the coast from Rio south to the northern portions of the state of São Paulo. There is a natural hybrid reported between *L. crispa* and *L. lobata* where their ranges cross, *L. wyattiana*. The natural hybrid, *Lc. amanda*, results from crossing with *C. intermedia*.

Fig. 56. *Laelia lobata* var. *alba.*

Long-peduncled Laelia

Brazil

Laelia longipes Reichenbach f. 1863. *Xenia Orch.* II, p. 59.
    Subgenus: *Parviflorae*
        Section: *Liliputanae*

Synonyms
Bletia longipes Reichenbach f. 1863. *Xenia Orch.* II, p. 59.
Bletia lucasiana Rolfe. 1893. *Orchid Review* 1: 265.

The 4–5 cm. long peduncle and ovary of the individual flower makes this species unique. The flower stalks are about 8 cm. high, the pseudobulbs 2–4 cm. and the leaves 3–5 cm. more, though with less light in cultivation the plants may grow a little larger. The color of the flowers is a rosy purple or lilac with a tendency to have a darker central area in both sepals and petals, not the more usual petal-only flare. If the lip is pulled down from its attachment, the prominent green nectary is apparent at the base of the column. The flower stalk has the same length relative to the leaf, which places the species with the other lilliputians.

The throat and disc of the flowers are cream colored, while the midlobe is margined and tipped with rose-purple. Only one or two flowers are produced. They bloom in October–November in Brazil in the Serra do Cipó. Hamilton's data show a concentration of flowering in September–October, other bloomings around July in the north. Better identifications and more data would resolve these discrepancies.

The dorsal sepal measures, in my specimen, 8 × 23 mm., the lateral sepals 9.5 × 17 mm., the petals are 9 × 23 mm., and the lip is 15 mm. long and 14 mm. wide. The ovary and pedicel at 4.6 cm. are the outstanding feature of the flower, approached only by yellow-flowered *L. itambana* with 4 cm. and lavender-purple *L. duveenii* with 3–4 cm., all the other miniature species being 3 cm. or less, regardless of their flower color. According to Cunha Filho's (1966) research in Brazil, *longipes* is the congener of *crispata* (*rupestris*), though by current classification systems these species would fall into different sections of the *Parviflorae*.

Fig. 57. *Laelia longipes.*
Form with pronounced color pattern.
Photo by Paul Gripp.

Fig. 58. *Laelia lucasiana.* On rock in Brazil. Photo by Trudi Marsh.

Lucas's Laelia

Brazil

Laelia lucasiana Rolfe. 1893. *Orch. Rev.* 1: 285.
Subgenus: *Parviflorae*
Section: *Liliputanae*

Synonyms
Laelia ostermeyeri Hoehne. 1938. *Arq. Bot. Estado São Paulo* 1(1): 19.
Laelia longipes var. *fournieri* Cogniaux. 1897. *Chron. Orch.*, 4: 29.

At one point the epithet of this taxon was considered a synonym of *L. longipes*, but it has now been raised to species rank. Prof. Garay, studying Rolfe's type specimen of *lucasiana*, found that *L. ostermeyeri* was the same thing. The variety *fournieri* turned out to be the white form of the species, not a natural hybrid of *L. longipes* × *L. flava*, as Hoehne originally considered it to be. The flowers of this species are easily recognized by their purple or magenta sepals and petals with which the golden lip makes such a distinct contrast. Inside the base of the throat there is a purple spot. Two other species also have distinctive yellow lips, *L. gardneri* and *L. reginae*, though in the latter the yellow is somewhat subdued.

The flowers measure 3–4 cm. in diameter, and the small plants are about 9–10 cm. high with a 5–6 cm. high flower stalk, about the same height as the leaves. The flowers bloom from October–December at about 1500 m.

in various mountains of Minas Gerais such as Serra de Ouro Preto, Serra da Piedade and Serra do Caraça.

Flower measurements show the dorsal sepal 8 × 24 mm., lateral sepals 8 × 21 mm., petals 7.5 × 22 mm. The lip is 14 mm. long and wide. The plants are a clear olive green color without red flushes. The species is named after C. J. Lucas, Warnham Court, Horsham, who purchased the plant in 1892 at Stevens' Rooms.

Fig. 59. *Laelia lucasiana.* White forms were originally identified as var. *fournieri.* Photo by Trudi Marsh.

Lund's Laelia

Brazil

Laelia lundii Reichenbach f. 1881. *Otia Bot. Hamb.* II, p. 92.
    Subgenus: *Microlaelia*

Synonyms
Bletia lundii Reichenbach f. and Warm. *ex* Reichenbach f. 1881. *Otia Bot. Hamb.* II, p. 92.
Laelia regnelli Barb. Rodr. 1882. *Gen. et Spec. Orch. Nov.* 2: 154.
Laelia reichenbachiana Wendland and Kraenzlin. 1892. *Xenia Orch.* III, p. 97, t. 254.

This laelia was ignored in both Veitch and Williams, not to mention *Curtis's Botanical Magazine* or Schlechter, although it was known from 1881 in the botanical literature. It is an unusual laelia and certainly belongs in its own subgroup, lacking any really close relatives, but that is usually reason to have taken up a species in order to describe it in detail. Whatever the problems may have been, it was described in the *Orchid Review* for February, 1910, (18:62–63) by Rolfe, who mentions certain confusions about its origins and classification.

The epithet *L. cattleyoides,* once a synonym but not in the list of synonyms above, is best applied to a natural hybrid between this species and *Cattleya loddigesii* collected originally by Richard Doering. I have not yet discovered how Lund or Regnell were connected with the discovery of the species, but Cogniaux in *Martius' Flora Brasiliensis* describes *cattleyoides,* *lundii* and *regnellii,* all three, as separate species. Hoehne combines the latter two in his *Iconographia* (1949) but no mention is made there of *cattleyoides.* I have also not yet discovered who made the combination *lundii* var. *regnelli*, perpetrating the idea that there was some sort of difference from the type. There is not, and the use of that epithet should be dropped. At most, that name should have been applied to a particular clone.

The creeping habit of this species is distinct among the laelias. It apparently inhabits thickets along the coastal mountains from Minas Gerais south toward São Paulo in the same habitat as *Cattleya loddigesii*, leading to their natural hybrid, *Lc. cattleyoides.* The *L. lundii* plants form spherical masses about the branches of small trees. The pseudobulbs are smooth, scarcely thickened and about 3–5 cm. apart as the plant marches across the substrate or grows out into the air, producing an ample supply of roots along the bottom side of its rhizomes.

Each growth has two leaves, 3–5 cm. long, that are nearly terete, actually somewhat triangular in cross-section, and come to a sharp point. This character is also unique among the Brazilian laelia species, all other Brazilian species producing single leaves on mature growths. The short flower stalk produces 1–3 flowers, usually one, among the leaves. They are a pristine white with dark red-purple veining on the lip. The veins make an almost solid pigmentation on the disc before they flare out toward the frilled margin of the lip. The flowers are usually produced on immature growths as the leaves begin to unfold.

Laelia lundii does not have much variability, and no varietal forms are described. The species has been used to produce a few hybrids and will be used more in the present quest for miniature orchids. They transmit their tolerance and easy growing habits to their progeny so that they have much to offer in addition to their miniature stature.

Fig. 60. *Laelia lundii.* Photo by Trudi Marsh.

Fig. 61. *Laelia mantiquierae.* Photo by Trudi Marsh.

Mantiqueira Laelia

Brazil

Laelia mantiqueirae Pabst. 1975. *Bradea* 1 (47):472 and 2(6):24.
Subgenus: *Parviflorae*
Section: *Rupestres*

Synonym
L. crispilabia Auct. non A. Richard.

This laelia has been recognized for some time but not really understood until Pabst's research in the species of this complex. The difficulty
revolved around an illustration labeled *L. crispilabia* in Cogniaux and
Goosens's *Dictionaire Iconographique des Orchidees* that was, in reality, *L.
mantiqueirae.* Comparison of the picture details with the type of *L. crispilabia*
in the Paris Herbarium revealed the differences, allowing Pabst to give this
species a proper name. Both species have a similar habit of growth, and
both produce rosy lavender or purple flowers, so the confusion was
understandable.

The lip midlobes of the two species are completely different, that of *crispilabia* being stalked and elongated, this species being unstalked and round. The disc and throat are a pale white or creamy color and the veining suffuses the lateral lobes with rosy purple, while the edges of the lateral lobes and the margins of the lip are a darker tone. Flower measurements are: dorsal sepal 7 × 25 mm.; lateral sepals 7 × 20 mm.; petals 6.5 × 25 mm.; lip 17 mm. long × 14 mm. wide when flattened.

This is apparently a widespread species as rupicolous laelias go, since it is found in a triangle between São João del Rei, Ouro Preto and Piedade in Minas Gerais. It is named after the Serra da Mantiqueira range of mountains. The plants flower in Brazil in September–November depending upon their elevation around 1000 m. They seem to flower in late winter–early spring in the Northern Hemisphere, according to Hamilton's data, but it is possible that some of the plants Hamilton used were those of mislabeled *crispilabia*. The pseudobulbs reach 6–7 cm., and the leaf—dark glaucous green, red-flushed and with a roughened surface—is 11–12 cm. long.

The possibility also exists that this species is the same as *L. caulescens* (please see). Until we understand these species in greater detail, they are best treated separately.

Miller's Laelia

Brazil

Laelia milleri Blumenschein. 1960. *Publ. Cient. Inst. Gen. ESALC* 1:38.
    Subgenus: *Parviflorae*
    Section: *Parviflorae*

This laelia took orchidists by storm when it appeared on the scene in 1962–63, so much so that Gordon Dillon asked me to write a short article about it for the *American Orchid Society Bulletin* because of my earlier visit to Brazil; it appeared in the February, 1964, issue. My first look at this laelia was in 1960 when Lester McDonald sent me a plant from McLellan's for identification. They had received a shipment of *L. flava* from Brazil, only to find that about half of them had red flowers instead of yellow. Needless to say, they were much excited about these plants, and McLellan's called them *L. flava* var. *aurantiaca* for lack of a better name at the time.

After my Guggenheim Fellowship trip in the fall of 1962 where I saw about 200 of the plants in flower at Orquidário Binot, I was finally able to ascertain the correct name. We earlier had met Almiro Blumenschein, one of Prof. F. G. Brieger's students, in Piracicaba at the state agricultural school where a large research collection of orchids was maintained. He gave me some of his publications, one about three new laelias, including *L. milleri*, named in honor of H. Miller for his contributions to the study of genetics in Brazil.

Vegetatively the plants are similar to those of *L. flava*, as the above confusion in the McLellan shipment indicates. The red pseudobulbs are up to 6 cm. high, widest at the base, and bear a stiff, somewhat narrow, 10 cm.,

Fig. 62. *Laelia milleri.* One of the darker, redder forms.

ovate leaf with a sharp tip. The leaf is borne at an angle to the pseudobulb, not in line with it, and the foliage of most plants has a deep maroon flush, particularly on the backs of the leaves.

The outstanding feature, of course, is the blood- or orange-red starry flower that can approach 5 cm. in diameter. They are produced on a tall stalk well above the leaves, as many as six in succession. The lip is yellow with cinnabar-colored veining. In Brazil I had noted two color types among the plants I had observed. One group had narrower sepals and petals, slightly larger flowers and an orange-red color. The other group had slightly smaller flowers with wider sepals and petals and their color was more a blood-red. I observed no flowers that combined the larger size with the darker color and wider segments. A typical flower measures: dorsal sepal 6.5 × 30 mm.; lateral sepals 7 × 25 mm.; petals 7 × 28 mm.; lip 18 mm. long, 12 mm. wide.

Laelia milleri flowers in November and December in Brazil, and in May through July when transplanted to northern countries. Of all the rock laelias, this species may be the closest to extinction in the wild—some collectors say it is already extinct. The area where it grows near Itabira in the Serra dos Ingleses in Minas Gerais has been strip-mined for iron ore leaving little or nothing of the species' natural rocky environment on iron ore outcroppings. Although the flowers have been used many times for their contribution of red to various crosses, no particular attempts have been made to raise the species itself from seed, for which it is a deserving candidate.

Fig. 63. *Laelia mixta.*

Mixed Laelia

Brazil

Laelia mixta Hoehne *ex* Ruschi. 1938. *Arq. Bot. Estado de São Paulo* 1(1):20,
t. 12 (Hoehne). 1946. *Arq. Publico do Espírito Santo,* p. 37, t. 41. (Ruschi).
    Subgenus: *Parviflorae*
        Section: *Parviflorae*

Here we have another taxonomic problem, but it is not as tormenting as *L. malletii* (discussed in Chapter 3). There was no type specimen, Pabst and Fowlie state, but there was a reasonable description by Ruschi who republished Hoehne's epithet with proper documentation, removing the name from its *nomen nudum* status. Hoehne originally believed that the plant was a natural hybrid of *L. flava* or *gloedeniana* and *L. harpophylla*, but that notion has now been discarded as natural populations of the plants have been discovered.

Since the flower drawing shows a definite stalk or foot to the midlobe, and there are well-spaced yellow flowers borne on a stem up to 65 cm. tall, it properly belongs with the group of *L. flava* relatives. The sheath is as much as 15 cm. long. Up to 15 flowers are produced per stalk. The throat and stalk of the midlobe is whitish or a pale cream color compared with the rest of the flower, and the veins show up as a darker color, almost reddish, on the yellow sepals and petals. The petals are about 30 mm. long, and the lip is about 14–15 × 20 mm. as measured from the sketch of the type. No actual flower measurements are given in the original descriptions.

Plants were collected at Pedra da Onca in Espírito Santo by Dr. Luciano Zappi, and one of the flowers is illustrated in color in the fine reprint on this group published by the Orchid Digest Corporation. They grow at about 800 m. and above, and were also found near Itaguaçu, Alfonso Claudio, Colatina and Cachoeira.

The pseudobulbs are thickened at the base and tapered to their tip, from 15–35 cm. high, and the leaves are 10–20 cm. long. The species was rediscovered, after Hoehne's original description, by Roberto Kautsky, an orchid enthusiast and grower, in company with Dr. Zappi. Most of the area originally described as habitat for this species is now under cultivation, it is stated, but the very arid Pedra da Onca still harbored the plants.

Ruschi's drawings for the type description are illustrated in the *Orchid Digest* for March–April, 1979.

Perrin's Laelia

Brazil

Laelia perrinii Lindley. 1842. *Bot. Reg.* 28, sub t. 62.
    Subgenus: *Crispae*
        Section: *Perriniae*

Synonyms
Cattleya perrinii Lindley. 1838. *Bot. Reg.* 24, t. 2.
Cattleya intermedia var. *angustifolia* Hooker. 1839. *Bot. Mag.*, t. 3711.
Cattleya integerrima var. *angustifolia* Hooker. 1846. *Cent. Orch.* 33, t. 30.
Bletia perrinii (Lindley) Reichenbach f. 1861. *Walp. Ann. Bot.* 6:421.

This well-known laelia had already been introduced into cultivation when Lindley named it in 1838 as a *Cattleya*, later changing part of the genus to *Laelia*. He did not know much about its origins in cultivation except that it was sent to Harrison in Liverpool from Rio de Janeiro and was named after Harrison's gardener, Perrin. It came from the Organ Mountains near Novo Friborgo. It was later collected in Minas Gerais at an altitude of about 700–900 m. and also has been found growing in Espírito Santo.

The flowers have several distinctive features. The narrow petals stand stiffly but droop a few degrees from vertical so that there is a wide separation from the dorsal sepal. The petal midrib can be prominent. The lateral sepals seem close together and are distinctly falcate (sickle-shaped), a characteristic more often associated with multifoliate cattleyas than with the laelias. The column is also unusual, being distinctly "sway-backed", arching into a curve, and tapering from the base into a narrow apex. It is not like any other column among the Brazilian cattleya-like laelias. The ovary is plump, swollen due to the larger-than-ordinary nectary inside. The bracts on new growths may be distinctly inflated instead of tightly surrounding the new stem and leaf. This species is therefore given its own section of classification as a consequence of its combination of unique characteristics.

The flowers are about 12–15 cm. across, and the color can range from a pale rose-purple, through a "diluted magenta-rose", to a darker purple. The white of the throat contrasts sharply with the darker velvety purple color of the midlobe. One or two flowers are usually produced, but as many as five have been reported. Often the blossoms have a sort of gray tone, and it is not unusual to find blue or "coerulea" types in the population. White forms are also known: one was called *alba*, another *nivea*. The plants in

Fig. 64. *Laelia perrinii.*

nature can form large masses, the pseudobulbs up to 25 cm. high with the leaves 25–30 cm. more. The leaves may be spotted on the reverse with purple mottlings.

The plants bloom in October and November in cultivation. They have been used a number of times to make various hybrids. *Laelia lilacina* is the natural hybrid of *L. crispa* × *L. perrinii. Laelia oweniae* is another natural hybrid, but the other parent is unknown and may be another *Laelia*, not a *Cattleya.*

Pfister's Laelia

Brazil

Laelia pfisteri Pabst and Senghas. 1975. *Die Orchidee* 26:253–255.
Subgenus: *Parviflorae*
Section: *Rupestres*

This is a purple-flowered laelia with elongated flower stalks but with flowers smaller than usual for section *Rupestres*. These flowers are only about 2.2 cm. across, are spaced relatively widely on the stems, and bloom successively. So far, the plants are known only from the Serra da Sincorá in Bahia, also the home of *L. sincorana.* This species is named after Gerhard Pfister, an orchid enthusiast from Mannheim, who had made many trips to Brazil to rediscover localities for earlier described species and to introduce these species into Germany.

Fig. 65. *Laelia perrinii* var. *coerulea.*

These plants were originally found by Eddie Waras from São Paulo in October, 1974, on a trip west of Salvador going to Barra da Estiva and Itaete. The habitat was at 1300 m. and received no rain from December until the following July. There were no other orchids, only a few cactus growing in the area. No previous lilac- or purple-flowered laelias had been found in Bahia, only the yellow *L. bahiensis*, so it was not difficult to identify this as a new species.

The pseudobulbs are dark purple growing in the full sun, about 6 cm. high, stubby, being thicker at the base, but also thickened at the top. The rugose leaves stand upright, are purple on the back, 7 cm. long × 2.3 cm. wide. They seem to be thinner in substance and wider for their size than is usual in this group. The sheath is 9–10 cm. long. As many as eight flowers are produced along the flower stalk that is up to 30 cm. tall. The throat and disc of the midlobe are white with 4 main, purple veins. *Laelia pfisteri* is generally similar to *L. mantiqueirae* but has the distinct bulb shape, smaller flowers and the unique geographic distribution in Bahia.

Flower measurements in the type description are: dorsal sepal 5 × 17 mm.; lateral sepals 5 × 15 mm.; petals 4.5 × 17 mm.; lip 14 mm. long, 10–11 mm. wide. The sepals and petals on our specimen run about 20 mm., but are otherwise comparable.

Fig. 66. *Laelia pfisteri.* Photo by Ron Parsons.

Dwarf Laelia

Brazil

Laelia pumila (Hooker) Reichenbach f. 1853. *Flor. des Serres* 9:102.
      Subgenus: *Crispae*
         Section: *Hadrolaelia*

Synonyms
Cattleya pumila Hooker. 1838. *Bot. Mag.,* t. 3656.
Cattleya marginata Paxton. 1843. *Paxt. Mag. Bot.* 10:265.
Cattleya pinellii Lindley. 1844. *Bot. Reg.* 30, t. 5, fig. 1 and text. n. 9.
Cattleya pinellii var. *marginata* Beer. 1854. *Prakt. Stud. Orch.,* p. 214.
Bletia pumila Reichenbach f. 1861. *Walp. Ann. Bot.* 6:421.
Laelia praestans var. *nobilis* Lindley. 1898. *Sem. Hort.,* p. 304.

This laelia is a dwarf species often used in hybridizing to produce
miniature hybrids. Dwarfness is a distinctly dominant characteristic, but

Fig. 67. *Laelia pumila.*

unfortunately it has another dominant quality as well: the tendency for the dorsal sepal of the flower to reflex back of the plane of the other flower parts so as to leave an unseemly gap in the countenance of the bloom. Occasionally a good, flat flower is found which is much valued horticulturally. The plants have slender pseudobulbs and are one-leafed.

The petals tend to hang down or droop a little and curl back towards their tips, sometimes markedly, and the flowers—usually one, sometimes two—have down-curved stalks that tend not to rise above the leaves. But the sprightly, rosy purple color of the sepals and petals is attractive and sets off the lip. The tube tends to a white or flush of color on the outside and in the throat, and the bell of the expanded midlobe is deep rich purple. In some forms the bell is margined in white, a pattern that gave rise to the epithet of *C. marginata.* A band of color may accompany the central veining in the throat, and sometimes a yellow color is also associated with the throat area. Darker veinings in the purple areas are sometimes apparent. At the apex of the lip is an extra fullness or frill that is lighter in color and which sometimes divides the dark purple completely in half. The 3 or 5 central veins are thickened or raised but not strongly keeled like those in some of the other species of *Hadrolaelia.* The tip of the central vein terminates in a little tuft that is readily apparent protruding from the throat, a characteristic that by itself can help one identify the *pumila* flower.

Many color forms have been described with a range from white to "blue" and to rosy pink types, as well as the darker purple. There is much variation in the degree of the light central area at the apex of the midlobe, some types showing great contrast. Often the pigmentation along the three central, thickened veins is dark and extends out toward the apex of the lip in a pointed design upon the area of lighter color. The clone 'Black Diamond' is currently a superior form, and there is also a good *coerulea* type available; *delicata* forms are barely flushed with color and have pink lip markings instead of the dark purple.

Confusion as to the proper identification of the clones arises, however, between *pumila* and *spectabilis* (*praestans*), once they leave Brazil if the locality of specific origin is not provided. A glance through several current books will show misidentified plants with both species labeled *pumila*. This problem is discussed under the description of *L. spectabilis* (*praestans*). The sepal width, wide in *spectabilis* and narrow in *pumila*; the angle of the petals, at right angles to the axis of the dorsal sepal in *spectabilis* and usually more than a right angle in *pumila* so the petals "droop"; the relative diameter, degree of closure over the column and length of the tube of the lip; and the presence of the "tuft" remain the best criteria for distinction. Fowlie discusses this problem and also illustrates the distinctions in an article in the March–April, 1973, *Orchid Digest*. Also, please see the discussion in this book under *Hadrolaelia* in Chapter 1.

Plants of this species flower from September–November, the Northern Hemisphere equivalent to the Brazilian spring. They are native to the northern part of the state of Rio de Janeiro, and on into central Espírito Santo and Minas Gerais in the delta area of the Rio Paraiba and the Rio Doce, usually at high altitudes. They may be found on trees in swampy woods with some shade and high humidity from 600–900 m. Another report tells of plants growing in the "peat swamp zone" on the east side of Caparão ridge at 1100 m. Small trees bordering the swamps and covered with moss provide a perfect habitat for these laelias, their roots running along the mossy bark not far above the water. The plants prefer a semi-exposed niche with high humidity. The new growth flowers before the leaf matures, the leaf acting as a surrounding sheath for the developing flower bud.

One natural hybrid of this species with *C. dormaniana* is called *Lc. porphyritis*. Another natural hybrid is with *C. loddigesii, Lc. leeana*.

Fig. 68. *Laelia pumila* 'Black Diamond'. Photo by Trudi Marsh.

Fig. 69. *Laelia pumila* var. *coerulea*. Photo by Trudi Marsh.

Purple-stained Laelia

Brazil

Laelia purpurata Lindley. 1852–3. *Paxton's Fl. Gard.* 3:112, t. 96
    Subgenus: *Crispae*
        Section: *Crispae*

Synonyms

Cattleya brysiana Ch. Lem. 1852. *Jard. Fleur.* 3, misc. p. 50 and t. 275, 276.
    Not *L. brysiana* Ch. Lem. = *L. elegans*.
Cattleya purpurata Beer. 1854. *Prakt. Stud. Fam. Orch.*, p. 213.
Cattleya crispa var. *purpurata* Hort. *ex* Reichenbach f. 1858. *Xenia Orch.*
    1:176.
Laelia casperiana Reichenbach f. 1859. *Koch's Wochenschr. f. Gaert.* 2:336.
Bletia purpurata Reichenbach f. 1861. *Walp. Ann. Bot.* 6:423.
Laelia wyattiana Reichenbach f. 1883. *Gard. Chron.*, p. 426.

The number of synonyms for the "Queen of the Laelias" indicates how many color forms of this laelia have been found and named as species, Reichenbach alone involved in naming three. In Cogniaux's 1898 account of the species in *Martius' Flora Brasiliensis* 73 color forms or varieties are listed, and the number of named clones in Brazil today probably exceeds 150. In fact, in Santa Catarina, the main home state of this laelia, fall orchid shows are devoted only to the plants of this species. I would venture to say that at present no other orchid species has more named varieties in cultivation than *L. purpurata*. It exceeds those of any of the cattleyas, or any other genus for that matter, as well as I can determine in the literature. In the book, *Monografia da Laelia purpurata, suas variedades e seus hibridos*, by Ferdinand J. Krackowizer (1950), 53 pages of varietal descriptions, with 5–7 descriptions to a page, are required to describe all the cultivars of this species.

Krackowizer emphasizes that color is the principal criterion for naming a particular clone but that other factors also enter the picture: the pattern of the color, the form of the flower and size as well as other charac-

Fig. 70. *Laelia purpurata* 'Schusteriana'. Photo by Jorge Verboonen.

teristics. His diagram of the lip, republished here (Fig. 73), shows the lip pattern where the colors typically vary. The same color variations appear on the other petals as well. Krackowizer goes on to classify all the color ranges in an effort to standardize color terminology for *purpurata*, included here as a chart in translation from the Portuguese (Table VIII). What other orchid, besides *C. labiata* in the recent work of Menezes, has had its variability so well documented?

Such an intense interest in the plants of this species has caused another kind of problem with a taxonomic twist for those interested in precise labeling of their plants in cultivation. That is the practice of grouping all the plants of a given color pattern under the same varietal name without further distinction as to specific cultivar. As I understand from my research, for example, there have been at least six or seven blue forms of this laelia found, and most all are called *L. purpurata* var. *werkhauseri* instead of each being given a separate clonal name, though Werkhauser himself, on finding a second blue clone, called it *werkhauseri* 'Superba'. Add to this difficulty the complication of the selfings and sib crossings that have resulted in many additional blue clones, for which the original varietal (clonal, cultivar) name is no longer a valid designation for a single plant without the addition of yet another name. Since the latter is not always done, it is almost impossible to tell whether the plant is a division of what was once a wild plant or whether it came from seed in cultivation. And if it was a wild plant originally, which one of the six or seven blues was it? Details such as these become of great importance when dealing with an orchid species with so many cultivar names and so popular in collections. Both Johnson and Verboonen note various forms of skulduggery Brazilian growers have undertaken in the past to keep "their" varieties unique. But now, through

Fig. 71. *Laelia purpurata.* 'Marie Louise'. Photo by Trudi Marsh.

Fig. 72. *Laelia purpurata* var. *carnea.* Photo by Ron Parsons.

mericloning by companies such as the Equilab in Brazil, many of the cultivar types, we hope properly labeled, are available through commercial growers in the United States and elsewhere. If a particular plant is to be used as a breeding parent, the clonal name immediately becomes of specific interest.

The flowers can be large, up to 25 cm. across, but the sepals and petals are often quilled or reflexed along their midribs and curled around at their tips so that a flat flower with straight segments is not easy to find. The usual number of flowers is 3–5 but as many as 7–8 are recorded. The plants may be massive, nearly 1 m. tall when growing well, half leaf and half pseudobulb. The type flower has white or nearly white sepals and petals and a lip that is white at the base and tipped with a strong purple "ring" on the bell, a semialba type of pattern when found occasionally among cattleyas, but here the norm. All purple forms, as one would find ordinary among cattleyas, are given special varietal names when found in this species. There is usually a veined area inside the throat that is yellow, even in forms that are otherwise white, and there is also a lighter color at the apex of the lip that sometimes splits the color "ring" where the veins from the throat begin to spread out over the disc. Such a split "color ring" pattern can also be found on the lips of *L. pumila* and *L. spectabilis* (*praestans*).

Flowers of this species have been used since the beginnings of orchid hybridizing; the first volume of *Sanders' Lists* itemizes 97 hybrids with *L. purpurata* as one parent. There are, of course, many more today, as this species is one of the mainstays of many of our present exhibition quality hybrids of six and seven generations. The twists and turns of the sepals and petals have long since disappeared, flattened out by the genetics of cattleyas, but the vigor of the plants, the flower size and the purple rim or "ring" on the lip can remain in their "great-grandchildren".

Laelia purpurata is found in the coastal areas, the littoral, of Brazil from just south of Rio de Janeiro into São Paulo state, through Santa Catarina and on into Rio Grande do Sul. It was also found on coastal islands such as Santa Catarina where this species had hybridized naturally with *C. intermedia* and *C. leopoldii*, as was discussed in Volume I of this series on cattleyas. The plants were once so common they were said to grow even in the sands along the beaches, but now they are found only on tall trees where they are out of reach except for the most heroic collector. They demand good light and air and an open sort of potting medium, and flower in late spring and early summer.

Plants were sent by Francois Devos to Verschaffelt in Ghent in 1847, Devos having found them in 1846 in southern Brazil. One of the plants found its way to the collection of James Backhouse and Sons in England. When it flowered and was exhibited at the Horticultural Society in 1852, it created a sensation as a new "*Cattleya*" and was described by Lindley, but properly as a *Laelia*.

An unusual point about the distribution of this species has been noted by Hoehne, Verboonen and others. It is not to be found in the state of Paraná, though it is found in Santa Catarina to the south and in São Paulo toward the north. This gap in the distribution along coastal Brazil is explained by the ancient geological history of Brazil, back to the Miocene-Pliocene periods when South America consisted of four major land masses separated by seas: the Northern and Southern Andean Cordilleras, the Guianan Shield and the Brazilian Planoalto or Highlands. Ancient seas must have covered that area now called Paraná, disrupting the range of this species and, in fact, producing the current disjunction in distribution.

Verboonen further notes that plants of *L. purpurata* from the southern portions of its range flower earlier than the plants from the north. If one moves them both to the same area, they continue to flower at different times, showing that this is a genetic, not an environmental, control. The late-bloomers all came from the state of Rio de Janeiro, the northern limits of distribution, and include many of the currently popular cultivars. Many are pictured in a recent article by Diekmann and Zschenker in *Die Orchidee* (May/June, 1989). See also Birck, p. 90, in the same issue for an explanation of the color varieties.

The following list of "varietal" categories indicates some of the color range among the plants of this laelia population and helps sort out many of the named clones and color patterns now offered for sale. Do remember, however, that the presence of one of these names on a label (see above) may not indicate a particular clone, only a particular color pattern.

aço—lip violet, sepals and petals white.
alba—pure white except for yellow in throat.
amena—sepals and petals white with tip of lip pink or rose.
anelata—ringed throat pattern with distinct veining on disc.
atropurpurea—sepals and petals dark rose, lip magenta-purple.
carnea—white with flesh-colored veining and lip.

coerulea—blue tones in veining and on lip.

delicata—excellent form and light color, a type of *amena* (*amoena*).

flamea—with a flame or flare on petals.

mandayana—good form and light pink-purple on lip, like a *russeliana*, but no veining in the throat.

marginata—with a white border around the lip.

oculata—having two eyes, the ringed color pattern broken in two by the central light color of the midlobe.

rosea—sepals and petals a light rose, lip darker, no yellow in throat.

roxo-bispo—dark purple of church robes.

russeliana—lip rosy lilac with pale rose at the throat.

sanguinea—blood red color in veins and on lip, sepals and petals.

striata—with striped petals.

venosa—veins show as stripes on lip.

vinho—wine-colored labellum.

vinicolor—wine-colored

werckhauseri—slate blue lip with blue-black veining.

Since this species covers such an extensive range, 800 or more kilometers along the coastal areas of southern Brazil, it is not surprising that natural hybrids between this species and other orchids have been found:

× *Cattleya forbesii* is *Lc. cypher*

× *C. leopoldii* is *Lc. elegans*

× *C. intermedia* is *Lc. schilleriana*

Synonyms of *Lc. elegans* are listed under the discussion of that hybrid species (as *L. elegans*) in earlier pages of this volume.

TABLE VIII

A standardized classification of colors used in describing forms of *Laelia purpurata* (Translated from Krackowizer, 1950)

Group 1. White colors
   a. translucent, "glass-clear"
   b. snow-white
   c. lightly tinged with yellow
   d. lightly tinged with ocher or cream
   e. washed with rose
   f. washed with lilac

Group 2. Rose to carmine colors
   a. bright rose
   b. rose
   c. carmine-rose
   d. color of currants
   e. color of pomegranate
   f. blood-red
   g. carmine
   h. carmine tinted with lilac
   i. dark carmine-violet

Group 3.　Violet to purple colors
     a. bright wine-color
     b. bright violet
     c. violet
     d. dark wine-color
     e. purple-violet
     f. dark purple tinged with violet
     g. deep purple, almost black

Group 4.　Lilac to lavender-blue colors
     a. bright lilac lightly tinged with blue
     b. bright lilac-gray
     c. slate-gray tinged with lilac
     d. lead-gray tinged with blue
     e. blue-gray tinted with lilac
     f. blue-gray
     g. dark blue-gray tinted with lilac

Group 5.　Ivory to maroon—maroon colors
     a. ivory
     b. bright ocher
     c. ocher
     d. flesh-colored
     e. cherry-colored
     f. pumpkin-colored
     g. brick-colored
     h. dark brick-red tinged maroon
     i. maroon tinted with violet

Group 6.　Yellow colors
     a. bright yellow
     b. lemon-yellow
     c. sulfur-yellow
     d. peach-colored
     e. canary-yellow
     f. egg yolk-yellow
     g. orange
     h. golden-orange
     i. dark gold color

Group 7.　Green Colors
     a. bright emerald-green
     b. green

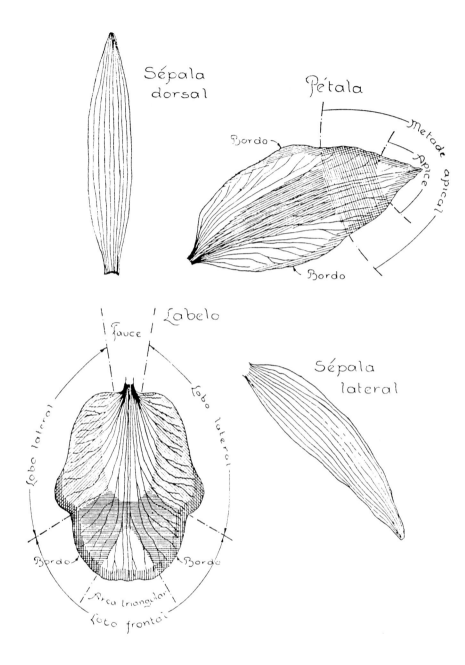

Fig. 73. *Laelia purpurata*. Diagram of the color pattern areas of the flower. From Krackowizer, 1950.

Fig. 74. *Laelia reginae.* Photo by Trudi Marsh.

Regina's Laelia

Brazil

Laelia reginae Pabst. 1975. *Bradea* 2(6):21–24.
Subgenus: *Parviflorae*
Section: *Liliputanae*

This tiny laelia is named after Regina Angerer, who flowered the type specimen in cultivation after she discovered it while collecting in the Serra da Caraça in Minas Gerais. Odebrecht (1988) describes finding it also near Belo Horizonte. It was the second species of the *Liliputanae* with a yellow lip, the other being *L. lucasiana* described in 1893 by Rolfe. A third species with yellow lip is *L. gardneri* in the *Rupestres*. The yellow of the *reginae* lip is somewhat subdued or obscured by the rosy purple flush on the veins and edge of the lip, but in the albescent forms it shows up clearly. The sepals and petals are a pale pink-purple or rose-lilac. Usually one flower is produced, but two sometimes appear.

The pseudobulbs are conical, 2–3.5 cm. high, and the succulent, channeled, stiff leaves are 3–4 cm. long × 1.6 cm. wide, somewhat roughened and with purple flushes on the back. The flower stalk is 2–4 cm. and the sheath 2–2.5 cm. long. The dorsal sepal is 4.5 × 14 mm.; the lateral sepals are 5 × 10 mm.; the petals 4 × 13 mm.; and the lip 7 mm. long × 9 mm. across when flattened.

The species is a charming miniature; one or two diminutive hybrids have already been produced with it.

Fig. 75. *Laelia reginae.* White form. Photo by Trudi Marsh.

Fig. 76. *Laelia rubescens.* Usual pale form. Photo by Trudi Marsh.

Fig. 77. *Laelia rubescens.* Rose-colored Oaxacan form.

Rosy-tinted Laelia

México, Guatemala, El Salvador, Nicaragua, Honduras, Costa Rica and
Panama

Laelia rubescens Lindley. 1840. *Bot. Reg.* 26, Misc. p. 17, 20, t. 41
    Subgenus: *Laelia*
        Section: *Podolaelia*

Synonyms
Laelia acuminata Lindley. 1841. *Bot. Reg.* 27, Misc. p.17, t. 24.
Laelia peduncularis Lindley. 1842. *Ibid.* 28, Misc. p. 9.
Laelia pubescens Lemoine. 1852. *Jard. Fleur.* 2: Misc. p. 79, 99.
Laelia violacea Reichenbach f. 1854. *Bonplandia* 2:89.
Cattleya acuminata (Lindley) Beer. 1854. *Prakt. Stud. Fam. Orch.,* p. 208.
Cattleya peduncularis (Lindley) Beer. 1854. *Ibid.,* p. 213.
Cattleya rubescens (Lindley) Beer. 1854. *Ibid.,* p. 214.
Bletia rubescens (Lindley) Reichenbach f. 1861. *Walp. Ann. Bot.* 6:425.
Bletia peduncularis (Lindley) Reichenbach f. 1861. *Ibid.* 6:426.
Bletia violacea (Rchb. f.) Reichenbach f. 1861. *Ibid* 6:426.
Bletia acuminata (Lindley) Reichenbach f. 1861. *Ibid.* 6:427.

This laelia has been given a real spectrum of names reflecting its wide
range of distribution and variety of color forms—from the typical
rubescent pink shading to plain white. In all of the color intergrades, how-

Fig. 78. *Laelia rubescens* var. *aurea.* Photo by Trudi Marsh.

ever, the dark maroon patch towards the base of the lip is constant. The quality of form is also highly variable. Some flowers are stringy and hardly open, others have wide petals and an overall good shape with open blooms. A fine flower will measure 6–7 cm. across, while others are considerably smaller, especially some of the white forms. Some of the brightest pink types with best form come from the neighborhood of Oaxaca, México. In spite of the species' long history from 1840 to the present, a rare yellow form has never been described.

The plants are short and tough and sometimes pigmented with purple when growing in the sun. It is a typical Méxican laelia in that it likes coolness, sun, good air, and a definite dormancy period in winter. The smooth, shiny pseudobulbs are somewhat compressed and oval in shape, around 3–5 cm. high, and there is one leaf, sometimes two, about 10 cm. long. The flower scape is 20–30 cm. high and bears 4–7 flowers near its top. The plants flower in midwinter in cultivation, and the flowers are fragrant.

When used as a parent in hybrids, the plant habit and the dark spot on the lip come through as dominant characters. The yellow blush seen on the disc in front of the dark area varies in intensity, and some plants toward the Pacific side of México have all-yellow instead of pink or white flowers.

The yellow forms are tentatively designated here as *Laelia rubescens* var. *aurea.* No doubt the Méxican researchers will have more to say about these yellow-flowered plants when they finish their research on this taxon and have sufficient herbarium material for type specimens and the proper valid publication of a name. I have seen a plant in flower in México, and one California orchid grower has had selfed seedling plants available for sale,

Fig. 79. *Laelia rubescens* var. *aurea.* Photo by Trudi Marsh.

so plants of this color should become more available in the future. They will undoubtedly have certain breeding potentials that hybridizers will notice. Since no other Méxican laelia has the size and color of this yellow variety, it will be much in demand. We hope that the yellow color might be a dominant characteristic in breeding; we know the deep color spot in the throat will be.

The type of *rubescens* was shown to Dr. Lindley in 1840 by Barker from Birmingham who had purchased a plant from what became the Veitch Nursery. No one knew of its habitat, however, until Hartweg rediscovered it in Guatemala. It is called *Flor de Jesus* by the country folk since it flowers November–December. It grows from sea level to about 1100 m. so is clearly a very tolerant species, helping to account for its wide range and variable nature.

It is interesting to note that Méxican *L. albida* also has a yellow variety, *sulphurea.* This parallel must have some significance, if only it could be fathomed. In 1987 Fred H. Strothmann of Edmond, Oklahoma, was awarded a C.C.M. for his *L. rubescens alba* 'Strothmann'. Not only was the plant well grown with 76 flowers and 165 buds on 24 inflorescences, but the flowers lacked the hallmark deep maroon spot in the throat, yellow remaining as the only color. This is so far the only plant in the history of this species to lack the spot, a rare occurence to say the least, and reminds me of the difficulty of finding white *C. skinneri* forms without darker color in the throats. Forms that are *alba-plena*, without even the yellow, are nearly unheard of in the cattleyas and laelias. The forms with the yellow spread throughout the flower are obviously not quite as rare.

Fig. 80. *Laelia sanguiloba.*

Red-lobed Laelia

Brazil

Laelia sanguiloba Withner. *Sp. nov.*

Pseudobulbis elongatis, teretibus, basi tumidis, purpureis, 3–4 articulatis, apice unifoliatis; foliis mediocribus patulis, crasse coriaceis, rugulosis, plus minusve concavo, subtus satis purpureis; pedunculo foliis multo longiore, superne 8–12 floro; floribus mediocribus, sepalis lanceolato-ligulatis, acuminatis, lateralibus paulo brevioribus, petalis similiter; labello valde recurvato, lobis lateralibus sanguinibus, lobo terminali aurantiaco, valde undulato-crispo, disco flavo. Withner *s.n. ex hort.,* Orquidário Binot, January, 1989. Plants from Bahia without exact location. Type deposited in Orchid Herbarium of Oakes Ames, Harvard University.

　　Subgenus: *Parviflorae*
　　Section: *Parviflorae*

This distinctive laelia is easily recognized by the blood-red lateral lobes of the lip. The flowers otherwise remind the grower of *L. cinnabarina,* though they are somewhat smaller than those of that species. The plant is similar to *L. flava* with slightly stouter pseudobulbs and more upright leaves, but with the same long-necked appearance. The bulbs and leaves are flushed deeply with red, and the leaves are tough, leathery and have a roughened surface. The plants are reported from Bahia, but without an exact location at present. They have been grown at the Orquidário Binot for a few years and have been called *L. flava* var. *micrantha* for lack of a better name. Although the plants are similar to those of *flava*, the flower structure indicates a closer affinity to *L. cinnabarina*. The type specimen was obtained by pressing one of the plants at the nursery, where a block of specimens was in full flower during January, 1989. Little variation was observed, the plants and flowers being similar from plant to plant, except for possible vigor of individual specimens and the numbers of flowers they produced.

The flower parts measure as follows: dorsal sepal 5.5 × 33 mm., lateral sepals 6.5 × 30 mm.; petals 6.5 × 35 mm.; lip 12 × 22 mm. overall when flattened, the lateral lobes 6 × 15 mm. and the terminal lobe 6 mm. wide × 7 mm. long from a stalked base about 5 mm. long. The red column measures 8 mm., and the ovary and its stalk measure 38 mm. Flowers on poor plants may be smaller, the petals only measuring 24 mm., with the other parts and numbers in proportion.

Flower stalks bear up to 12 flowers, are 38 cm. high and emerge from basal sheaths about 8 cm. high. The pseudobulb is 10 cm. tall, and the leaf measures 28 mm. × 145 mm.

The sprightly color, red lateral lobes, and generous flower production should make this a favorite species for both the grower and the hybridizer.

Sincora Laelia

Brazil

Laelia sincorana Schlechter. 1917. *Orchis* 11:72.
Subgenus: *Crispae*
Section: *Sincoranae*

Synonym
Cattleya grosvenori Ruschi. 1969. *Bol. do Mus. de Biol., Serie Bot.* 23:1.

Although this laelia was described many years ago, having been collected as early as 1906, it was not known in our collections until recently, seeming to have burst upon the scene about 10–15 years ago. Even in Brazil it was so poorly known that Ruschi described it as a new species as late as 1969 after he had "rediscovered" it. Since then orchidists have vied to acquire good clones, and it has been used in several hybrids to produce miniature orchids with large flowers. Its growth habit is much like that of a rock laelia, which it is not, but that is how it looks to a grower. The growths are short, tough, stubby, succulent and tightly clustered together. The leaf is concave, and the plants are purple in good light. One or two flowers are produced per growth, mostly in May in the Northern Hemisphere, December in Brazil.

The past connection of this species with *Hadrolaelia* is attributible to its generally dwarf habit and from the five keels or ridges extending down the center of the lip. The lip has distinct lateral lobes, however, that separate it from the *Hadrolaelia* species, and this characteristic, along with the growth habit, indicates a relationship with the rock laelias. It is therefore distinctive and cannot be confused with any other species. Accordingly, I place it here in its own section, *Sincoranae*, and separate it from *Hadrolaelia*, placing the new section ahead of the *Parviflorae*.

The flowers are a bright, rosy purple, darker on the lip and with yellow in the throat. As in *L. pumila* flowers, the dorsal sepal usually flares back, and the petals often tend to droop. The finest flowers are about 10–11 cm. across and have a distinct "cattleya" appearance.

The Serra da Sincorá in Bahia is a dry, barren, fossiliferous sandstone area supporting desert vegetation. Ruschi also found *L. sincorana* in the Serra do Capa Bode. The orchids grow at about 1100–1300 m. on *Vellozia* bushes, most of the rainfall coming from October–January, with hot, dry winds at other times of the year and a season with dense fogs and clouds. Occasionally the plants grow on the rocks in cracks and crevices. Obviously, they are well adapted to the desert-like environment. *Laelia bahiensis* and *C. elongata* may be found in the same general area.

Fig. 81. *Laelia sincorana* 'Ana Maria' AM/AOS. Photo by Trudi Marsh.

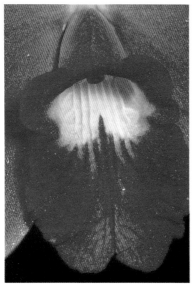

Fig. 82. *Laelia sincorana.*
Lip detail.
Photo by Trudi Marsh.

May-flowered or Showy Laelia

México

Laelia speciosa (Humboldt, Bonpland and Kunth) Schlechter. 1914. *Die Orchideen*, p. 233.
   Subgenus: *Laelia*
      Section: *Laelia*

Synonyms
Bletia speciosa Humboldt, Bonpland and Kunth. 1816. *Nov. Pl., Gen. and Species* 1:342.
Bletia grandiflora La Llave and Lexarza. 1825. *Nov. Veg. Descr.* 2: 17.
Laelia grandiflora (LaL. and Lex.) Lindley. 1831. *Gen. Sp. Orch. Pl.*, p. 115.
Laelia majalis Lindley. 1839. *Bot. Reg.* 25, Misc. p. 35.
Cattleya grahami Lindley. 1841. *Gen. Sp. Orch. Pl.*, p. 116.
Cattleya majalis (Lindley) Beer. 1854. *Prakt. Stud. Fam. Orch.*, p. 212.

Among the first New World orchids known to science, plants of this species were described by the Jesuit Hernandez in his illustrated natural history of New Spain published in 1615. Humboldt and his fellow explorers found them on the Pacific side of México between Acapulco and Playas de Coynca in Guerrero, and later La Llave and Lexarza found them in Michoacán. Don Herman (*Orchid Digest*, 1977) has written an interesting account on Humboldt and Bonpland and some of the plants they discovered. Plants were later found in other states around México City in the Central Plateau and highlands. It grows at high altitudes, as much as 2400 m., and is a hardy, cold-tolerant species, even surviving freezing temperatures for short periods.

The flowers are large and spectacular for the size of the plant, really *grandiflora*, the local people calling it *Flor de Mayo*, the May flower, that in Latin becomes *majalis*. It was gathered by the hundreds for celebrations, and plants were often naturalized in village dooryards. Stirling Dickinson, long a student of Méxican orchids, once took me collecting. After driving up a rough dry stream bed a couple of miles we found the plants growing on the rough bark of short, scrubby oak trees, almost completely exposed to the dry air, sun and winds. But there were festoons of Spanish moss hanging here and there, so the night humidity must have been fair. The laelias were very tough plants, difficult to pry off the bark. Stirling had long looked for a white form in the wild but never found one, though discovering on three or four occasions white clones naturalized around an old hacienda. They had evidently long been especially desirable finds, so any that have found their way into cultivation should be conserved carefully and seedlings raised from them.

The pseudobulbs are oval or rounded and the leaves 12–13 cm. long. There is one leaf, and one or two flowers about 16–17 cm. across are produced. The color is a vibrant pink-purple or rose-purple, the lip paler in the central areas and usually marked with rows of purple spots along the lateral veins. The border of the lip is a darker mauve-purple. There is a yellow band along the central main veins as they extend beyond the two-ridged callus at the base of the lip, a lip pattern not unlike that of *Cattleya maxima*. Unlike other Méxican species, this laelia does not have an elongated flower stalk with nodes, it being at most twice the height of the leaves.

Fig. 83. *Laelia speciosa.* Photo by Hugh Henry.

Speciosa in Latin means showy or splendid, and this species well fits that epithet. It is the type species for the genus *Laelia*, and a better species could not be found for representing this varied genus. It has been used for hybrids on a few occasions, but more use should be made of it for its small habit and large flowers, not to mention its cold tolerance. Its natural hybrid with *L. albida* is *L. eyermanniana*; and with *L. furfuracea, L. venusta.*

The main problem in growing *L. speciosa* seems to arise out of ignoring its definite winter dormancy. If watered liberally, it rewards the grower by rotting. Needless to say, it is best grown on a slab of cork or hung high near the glass in a basket with a maximum of light in a distinctly cool location.

Fig. 84. *Laelia speciosa* growing near San Miguel de Allende, México.

Spectacular or Distinguished Laelia

Brazil

Laelia spectabilis (Paxton) Withner (*comb. nov.*)
    Basionym: *C. spectabilis* Paxton. 1850. *The Florist* 3, p. 89, 91 with t.
    Subgenus: *Crispae*
        Section: *Hadrolaelia*

Synonyms
Cattleya pumila var. *major* Ch. Lemaire. 1859. *Ill. Hort., 6, t. 193.*
Bletia praestans (Rchb. f.) Reichenbach f. 1861. *Walp. Ann. Bot.* 6:425.
Laelia praestans Reichenbach f. 1857. *Allg. Gartenzeit.* 25:336.
Laelia pumila var. *mirabilis* Ed. Morren. 1878. *Belg. Hort.* 28:279, t. 17.
Laelia pumila var. *praestans* (Rchb. f.) Veitch. 1887. *Man. Orch. Pl.* II, p. 79.
Laelia pumila subsp. *praestans* (Rchb. f.) Bicalho. 1976. *Bradea* 2: 107–110.

This Distinguished Laelia is well named, for not only has it been recognized for its fine horticultural qualities, it has also caused a distinguished confusion as to its placement in the scheme of things. Some writers still consider it a form of *L. pumila,* including those currently in charge of R.H.S. policy which lumps the two species together. But it is often recognized as a separate species in other horticultural circles, though the distinctions between the two species seem to overlap, and care must be taken with proper identification. Then there is the question about its proper scientific name!

How may *L. spectabilis* and *L. pumila* be told apart? The differences are mostly relative, but useful enough. Flowers of *L. spectabilis* are larger and more striking in their quality than those of straight *pumila*, and the trumpet-shaped lip is broader and longer and tends to be arched or curved toward the "bell". This upward "cowhorn" sweep is readily apparent when the flowers are viewed from the side. There is no central "tuft" on the disc where the keeled veins run down onto the midlobe. Where the lateral lobes wrap together over the column they are stiff in texture and will split or crack if an attempt is made to open the lip for study. The petals are broader for their length than those of *pumila*, obtuse instead of tapered and pointed at their tips and not drooping in their general posture. Please read under *L. pumila* for additional comments; also see the discussion under *Hadrolaelia*.

Plants of *L. spectabilis* may have short, fat bulbs but many are thin and more pencil-like, this no doubt a response to the amount of light to which they are exposed. They are mostly one-leafed, but an occasional growth with two leaves has been seen. One or two flowers are produced per growth. The tight sheaths may cause a constriction around the center of a pseudobulb, an unusual happening illustrated in some of the old color plates. Flowers are produced on immature growths, the developing leaf functioning as a protective sheath for the bud, a characteristic of the whole Section.

Fig. 85. *Laelia spectabilis.* Photo by Jorge Verboonen.

The flowers are 10–13 cm. across, usually a rich deep rosy purple in color with the bell of the lip trumpet a deep dark purple. There is yellow in the throat around the three thickened central veins where they extend onto the disc. The balance of the throat is white or flushed with color as is the outside of the lip at its base. The purple is also apparent in the throat before the central veins emerge. Often there seems to be an extra frill at the apex of the lip that is a paler color than the rest, a feature also found in *L. pumila* and *L. purpurata*. Fowlie's illustrations of the columns of *spectabilis* (as *praestans*) and *pumila* in the March–April 1973 *Orchid Digest* also show distinctions: the column of *spectabilis* is comparatively short and wide, that of *pumila* long and narrow. The description of the habitat area in the same paper is excellent.

This was formerly a rare plant in collections, but recently it has been grown from seed and propagated by mericloning so that it is readily available. It was introduced to English collections as a chance plant in a batch of *L. pumila*, then known as *Cattleya marginata*, sent to Loddiges and exhibited at an R.H.S. Show under the name *C. spectabilis*. The plant Reichenbach actually described, however, flowered in the collection of Reichenheim in Berlin. It had come presumably from Santa Catarina at altitudes of 600–800 m. in southern Brazil. Other reports confirm Espírito Santo as a source, and still another the vicinity of Belo Horizonte in Minas Gerais. Fowlie says that it is found only near Belo Horizonte, but his friend Roberto Kautsky found it north of Domingos Martins. The local people call it *Mocinha de Labios Pintados*, the young girl with painted lips.

In the Minas Gerais locales the plants have been all but exterminated by the charcoal makers so that they only remain in rough places of difficult access between the Rio Velhas and the Rio Paraepebo. Some of these distribution discrepancies are no doubt the result of improper identifications, and details must be reconfirmed for accurate information. The plants prefer some shade and moist humid growing conditions, growing rather "deliberately" and never producing more than a few roots. In the Domingos Martins habitat the plants grow at 800–900 m. on southeastward facing ridges of mountains too steep for cultivation. There is high humidity with abundant moss and lichen development.

As plants gradually became known after introduction into various collections, including a lovely *alba* form in the W. Bull collection in Chelsea, various clones were singled out for varietal names. Cogniaux listed 20 named clones in *Martius*, but none of them are likely still extant, though others in the same categories, such as *alba*, may be purchased today. It is noted in the *Orchid Album* that when the plant is growing well in cultivation it may first flower in the spring and again on new growths in the late autumn. Hamilton's data show a main flowering in the fall.

The nomenclatural problem with this species is resolved with a search of the literature. If indeed the first plant in cultivation was named *Cattleya spectabilis*, then that epithet becomes the basionym for its proper scientific name. That would mean the epithet should be *Laelia spectabilis* (Paxton) Withner. An examination of the picture in *The Florist*, the accompanying text, and the note by Loddiges printed in the *Orchid Review*, p. 269, 1896, provide the evidence for this change. The use of *praestans* postdates Paxton's *spectabilis* by seven years, thus making *L. praestans* a synonym.

CATTLEYA SPECTABILIS.

Fig. 86. *Laelia spectabilis.* Type illustration as *Cattleya spectabilis, The Florist,* 1850.

Fig. 87. *Laelia tenebrosa* 'Raintree'. Photo by Peter Grinnell.

Dark Laelia

Brazil

Laelia tenebrosa (Gower) Rolfe. 1893. *Orch. Rev.* 1:146.
　　Subgenus: *Crispae*
　　　Section: *Crispae*

Synonym
Laelia grandis var. *tenebrosa* Gower. 1891. *The Garden* 1:36.

During its first few years in cultivation the plants of this species were known as *L. grandis* var. *tenebrosa,* indicating its dark color compared to the yellow of *grandis* flowers, but the term *tenebrosa* also implies something mysterious or supernatural, not just a comparison of color. Rolfe finally realized it was a separate species and described it while editor of the *Orchid Review*. Not only are the flowers a different color, but the plants and flowers are both larger than those of *L. grandis*. There is a similarity though in the veining pattern and the way color stands out in a ring on the lip that is similar to the flowers of both *purpurata* and *grandis*. This is, in fact, a typical pattern found in most species of section *Crispae*. Two or three flowers are usually produced per growth.

　　The flowers of this Dark Laelia have a bronze or coppery hue on the sepals and petals, and the lip has a deep purple ring with a lighter colored margin toward the apex. The throat is yellow and the veining prominent, extending out over the disc to the margin of the lip. They are handsome with a striking color pattern. Because of the flowers' relatively larger size and slightly more flattened petals, the species has been much used in hybridization. The genetic effect is the same as with dark bronzy cattleyas, such as *C. bicolor* or *C. leopoldii*—an intensification of pigmentation in the offspring. When used with *C. aurea* or *dowiana*, various shades of dark magenta—approaching red—have been produced, especially if the 'Walton Grange' cultivar had been used among the early antecedents.

It was thought until just a few years ago that this classic variety of the species had been lost to cultivation. Rita Crothers, in the Sept.–Oct. 1972 *Orchid Digest*, recounts her search of more than 20 years for the 'Walton Grange' clone that had originally been in the W. Thompson collection at Walton Grange in Stone, Staffordshire. It received a First Class Certificate from the R.H.S. on Aug. 8, 1893, the flowers of this clone departing considerably from the usual, mostly by lacking the customary bronzy coloration but, unusually, retaining a canary-yellow or citron background color with reddish tones in the ordinarily purple veining and lip ring. The other portions of the lip are white. The most recent illustration in color of this unusual clone is in the colorful *Quality Stream "Cattleyas"*, p. 25, with its superb photographs by the Japan Orchid Growers Association. In June, 1987, the clone was awarded an FCC/AOS of 91 points. One assumes from the photograph in the *Awards Quarterly* that this was for its color and history, not its very quilled and rolled sepals and petals.

The variety 'Rayon D'Or' seems to be a comparable clone, but little has been heard of it since it was illustrated last century in *Lindenia*. Collectors today should be on the lookout for a third or other yellow-flowered clones of this species. At present, the varieties 'Maria Fumaca' and 'Fujita', both with yellow-tan sepals and petals and red-purple veining on a white midlobe, are popular mericlones. Érico Machado in Espírito Santo has found two clones completely lacking any of the red or purple pigmentation, having yellow sepals and petals and a white lip.

Rolfe first saw a flower of this species in 1889 when Orquidário Binot shipped plants of it that year to Europe, the plants coming from the southern parts of Bahia and also Espírito Santo. They flower in our collection in summer. Two natural hybrids have been described. *Laeliocattleya cranstoniae* from Espírito Santo is a cross with *C. harrisoniana*, and *Lc. gottoiana* is a union with *C. warneri*, from the same state.

Fig. 88. *Laelia tenebrosa* 'Rayon D'Or'. *Lindenia,* plate 790, as *L. grandis* var. *tenebrosa* subvar. 'Rayon D'Or'.

Fig. 89. *Laelia tereticaulis.* Photo by Trudi Marsh.

Round-stemmed Laelia

Brazil

Laelia tereticaulis Hoehne. 1952. *Arq. Bot. Est. São Paulo* 3:163.
  Subgenus: *Parviflorae*
  Section: *Rupestres*

I remain unconvinced that this is a separate species, distinct from *L. crispata*, as Pabst and Fowlie list only a recurving of flower parts, slightly more falcate lateral sepals, more flowers and a later flowering season as the distinguishing characteristics. The flowering season is of particular importance, but there are apparently intergrades between the two types, and one of these forms is pictured in the *Orchid Digest* account of these species (Jan.–Feb., 1984). This could be a hybrid population of laelias beginning to separate into two separate taxa, but the degree of distinction is not yet great. So, for those who are interested, we'll follow Hoehne, Pabst and Fowlie, who have studied these plants and done more field observations on them than others, and who believe in their separateness. Additional studies may unquestionably prove their point.

Hoehne, in his type description, specifies the differences after repeated observations such as the length and round shape of pseudobulbs (from which its name is derived), the glaucous color of the leaves, the intense red-purple on the midlobe of the lip and the different sizes of the flower parts. How can all that not convince me?

The flowers are a rose-lilac or violet, and 7–9 are produced toward the top of a tall 42 cm. scape from mid–October–mid-December in Brazil. The plants are found in the Diamantina district of Minas Gerais and were first collected about 1947. The lip has a yellow throat and disc, and the dark intense red-purple apex is frilled and curled back in usual rock laelia fashion. There are white areas without the purple pigments at the bases of sepals and petals.

The plants are a gray-green color with their noticeable glaucous covering, the same as those of *L. crispata*, and may reach 20–50 cm. or more in height, the pseudobulbs reaching 20–30 cm. and leaves 15–22 cm. The spathe is 10 cm. long. The petals are 7 × 25 mm. long on my specimen, narrower than the sepals; dorsal sepal is 7.5 × 25 mm.; lateral sepals 7.5 × 21 mm.; and the lip is 14 mm. long × 12 mm. wide with two main veins. The ovary and its pedicel measure 45 mm., comparatively long, while in *L. crispata* they measure only 25 mm. The lip of this species seems small in relation to the size of the petals.

Green-flowered Laelia

Brazil

Laelia virens Lindley. 1844. *Bot. Reg.* 30, Misc. p. 1
Subgenus: *Crispae*
Section: *Crispae*

Synonyms
Laelia johniana Schlechter. 1912. *Orchis* 6: 6, t. 1.
Laelia goebeliana Küeppers and Kränzlin. 1916. *Ann. des k. k. Hofmus. in Wien* 30:56.

This is a very modest species and once seen is easily relegated to the back seat as far as laelias are concerned. One would include it in a collection only in the interest of having an example of every species in the genus. The sepals and petals are a pallid, creamy green, and often do not open even halfway before the flowers are on their way to produce seed pods. In other words, the blossoms are semi-cleistogamous and are not usually seen in an open state. The lip is white and slightly undulate. The flowers are

Fig. 90. *Laelia virens.*

small, about 2–3 cm. in size, the lip measuring 2.5 × 1.8 cm., and 5–6 may be produced in umbelloid racemes on a well-grown plant. The plants are of medium height, about 20–25 cm.

This species was thought to be a form of *L. xanthina* and was placed in synonymy with that species in earlier orchid studies so that it does not begin to appear "on its own" until about 1900 after Rolfe described it in the *Orchid Review*. Also, at one point, it was thought to be native to Colombia. It was ignored by Veitch, our usual source for early information, and Cogniaux lists it in synonymy in *Martius' Flora Brasiliensis*. Rolfe, however, tells us that it was originally discovered by Gardner in the Organ Mountains near Rio de Janeiro in 1837, and in 1844 it flowered in the Loddiges Nursery in Hackney, not "reappearing" until 1879 and then 1888, so it was never well known. In the 1914 first edition of Schlechter's *Die Orchideen* this species is listed as originating in Panama, as it is in the 1927 second edition, but in the third edition, currently being distributed, the geography has been corrected.

It is apparently not a common plant in nature and should not be confused with Reichenbach's 1858 name of *L. virens* that was a color form of *L. lobata*. To date it has not been used to produce any hybrids. The only other laelia species with partly open flowers is the newly found *L. alaorii* in the *Hadrolaelia* section of the genus because of its keeled lip. Although the flowers of *virens* don't really match in size and habit its other congeners in section *Crispae*, it still fits that taxon better than any other. It probably should be placed in its own section, but that seems to be excessive splitting at the present, producing another monotypic taxon in the genus.

Yellow Laelia

Brazil

Laelia xanthina Lindley *ex* Hooker. 1859. *Bot. Mag.,* t. 5144
Subgenus: *Crispae*
Section: *Crispae*

Synonyms
Bletia flabellata Reichenbach f. 1861. *Walp. Ann. Bot.* 6:422.
Bletia xanthina (Lindley *ex* Hooker) Reichenbach f. 1862. *Walp. Ann. Bot.*
6:425
Laelia wetmorei Ruschi. 1970. *Bol. Mus. Biol. Prof. Mello-Leitao, S. Bot.* 29:1.

The plants of this species grow about 30 cm. high and have smallish 7–9 cm. flowers to match. It is not one of the large, massively growing types of laelia that are its first cousins. But, like them, it has similar cultural requirements in liking good light, good drainage and an airy position in the greenhouse. In the *Orchid Album* there is mention of a fine specimen in the Shaw Collection that was 2 ft. (.65 m.) in diameter. It will grow well in a tree fern basket hung near the glass.

The flowers are a subdued yellow, the nankeen yellow of the older books, with a white lip and 3–5 red-purple veins from the throat onto the disc. The throat is yellow, and the lateral lobes do not close completely over the column. The anther cap is maroon at the tip of the white column. Petals and sepals may reflex along their midribs, but the shape can be somewhat flat. The pseudobulbs are distinctively narrowed at their bases, and the flower scapes bear 4–6 blooms. It has a pleasing aspect and has been used a few times in producing yellow or green hybrids.

The species name is derived from the Greek word for yellow, instead of the usual Latin designations, and emphasizes that yellow color is really not uncommon in this genus, especially when considering all the rupicolous species. Lindley could not have used the Latin *flava* to name this species as he had already used that term for *L. flava* that he described in 1839.

It was introduced into cultivation in the early years by Backhouse and Sons of York but was always a scarce plant. It comes from the same areas as *L. tenebrosa* and *L. grandis* in Bahia and Machado reports it from mountains in Espírito Santo. It was imported from Brazil about 1858, and Lindley described it the following year.

Fig. 91. *Laelia xanthina.*

Fig. 92. Unidentified *rupicolous Laelia*. Photographed at Orquidário Binot, January 1989.

CHAPTER 3

Questionable or Obscure Species

Mallet's Laelia

Brazil

Laelia malletii St. Leger. 1890. *A Cidade do Rio de Janeiro* 23:7.
Subgenus: *Parviflorae*
Section: *Liliputanae*

This laelia is really unknown except for its name so probably should not be listed. There is no way to find out now what it really was. The old description was published but only in generalities—it had purple flowers, 5–8 on a stalk, 5–7 cm. high. That would have meant flowers appeared at about the same height as the leaves, so it is tentatively placed here in section *Liliputanae* which has those qualities. There is no type specimen remaining to confirm the identity.

Since in all likelihood the taxon originally described is now called by another name, this one is hereby declared a *nomen nudum*. With the identity obscure, it is impossible to choose another type specimen to go with this name. That puts it in limbo, but the name will turn up in the literature when this group is studied in detail.

Orquidário Binot has plants of another small, yellow-flowered rupicolous laelia that would fall in section *Esalqueanae*. It appears close to *L. itambana*, but at the present time is not well enough understood to identify as a separate entity.

Fig. 93. Cattleya house at the Royal Exotic Nursery, King's Road, Chelsea. From Veitch (1887).

Selected References For Additional Information

Bicalho, Hamilton Dias. 1981. Contribuição do Departamento de Genética, ESALQ, USP, à orquidófila e orquidologia nacionais. In *Orquidófilos E Orquidólogos*, pp. 61–69. Rio de Janeiro, Brasil.

Bicalho, Hamilton Dias and Jiro Miura, eds. 1977. *Native Orchids of Brasil*. Associação Orquidófila de São Paulo. São Paulo, Brasil.

Birck, S. 1989. *Laelia purpurata. Die Orchidee* 40(3):94–98.

Blumenschein, Almiro. 1957. *Estudos Citólogicos na família Orchidaceae.* Doctoral thesis. 70 pp. plus graphs and tables. Escola Superior de Agricultura "Luiz de Queiroz", Universidade de São Paulo. Piracicaba, Brazil.

Blumenschein, Almiro. 1960. *Estudo sôbre a evolução no subgênero Cyrtolaelia (Orchidaceae).* 54 pp. plus drawings and tables. Thesis presented to Escola Superior de Agricultura "Luiz de Queiroz", Universidade de São Paulo for appointment to Chair of Cytology and Genetics. Piracicaba, Brazil.

Brieger, F. G, R. Maatsch and K. Senghas. 1981. *Schlechter's Die Orchideen.* Third Edition. Verlag Paul Parey. Berlin.

Cogniaux, A. 1898. Orchidaceae II, Tribus VII Laeliinae. In *Martius' Flora Brasiliensis*, Vol. 3, part 5.

Crothers, Rita. 1972. Search for a "lost" orchid—*Laelia tenebrosa* var. Walton Grange. *Orchid Digest* 36 (5):165–166.

Cunha Filho, L. A. da 1966. *Contribuição ao estudo da evolução do subgênero Cyrtolaelia (Orchidaceae) com base na determinação das distâncias generalizadas de Mahalanobis.* Master's thesis, ESALQ, 58 pp., Piracicaba, Brasil.

Diekmann, R. and L. Zschenker. 1989. *Laelia purpurata-Die wandelbare Königin. Die Orchidee* 40(3):79–84.

Duveen, Denis I. 1976. The experience of M. Forget with *Laelia jongheana. Orchid Digest* 40(2):55–57.

Duveen, Denis I. 1979. Some novelties among Brazilian orchids. Part VII.

Laelia mixta Hoehne ex Ruschi refound in Espírito Santo. *Orchid Digest* 43(2):73–75.

Duveen, Denis I. 1984. Some observations concerning the naming of Section *Parviflorae* Lindl. of the genus *Laelia. Orchid Digest* 48 (1): 11–12.

Ewald, Paulo. 1949. Orquídeas do Estado de Santa Catarina e seus híbridos naturais. *Orquidea* (Brazil) pp. 130–135.

Fowlie, J. A 1973. Three confused *Laelia* species from Brazil and their known varieties. *Orchid Digest* 37(2):63–71.

Fowlie, J. A 1974. With Ghillány in Brazil. Part VI. Rock-dwelling laelias in a most unique habitat. *Orchid Digest* 38 (2): 66–71.

Fowlie, J, A. 1977. In Brazil: Part XIII. In search of the missing *Laelia fidelensis* Pabst. *Orchid Digest* 41(4):147–149.

Fowlie, J. A 1980. In Brazil: Part XVII. *Laelia praestans* refound in eastern Espírito Santo by Robert Kautsky. *Orchid Digest* 44(3):113–117.

Fowlie, J. A 1981. Some additional notes on the rupicolous *Laelia* species of Espírito Santo in Brazil, including *Laelia gloedeniana* Hoehne and *Laelia blumenscheinii* Pabst. *Orchid Digest* 45(3):113–116.

Fowlie, J. A 1984. In Brazil: part XXIV. Albinism in the population of *Laelia sincorana* on vestigial plateaus of the Serra Sincora in Bahia. *Orchid Digest* 48(4):129–132.

Ghillány, Anton. 1974. New and rare Brazilian rupicolous laelias (introduction and the *Flavae*). *Am. Orchid Soc. Bull.* 43(3):227–234. Part II. (The *Flavae* completed) 43 (4):323–325. The *Lilacinae.* 43(11):989–995.

Hamilton, Robert M. 1986. *When Does It Flower?* 2nd. ed. Published by the author, Vancouver, B.C.

Herman, Don. 1977. Humboldt and Bonpland. *Orchid Digest* 41(4):133–138.

Hoehne, F. C 1958. Concerning the genus *Laelia* Lindl. of the *Orchidaceae* and its new species from the State of Minas Gerais. *Am. Orch. Soc. Bull.* 27 (6):400–402, 760–766, 842–846. This is a translation of the same article in Portuguese published in *Arquivos de Bot. do Estado de S. Paulo,* new series, 2 (6):157–167. 1952.

Johnson, C. E 1950. *Laelia purpurata* and its rare varieties. *Am. Orchid Soc. Bull.* 19(12):652–657.

Jones, H. G 1968. Studies in neotropical orchidology. *Acta Bot. Acad. Sci. Hungaricae* 14(1–2):63–70.

Krackowizer, Ferdinand J. 1950. *Monographia da Laelia purpurata, suas variedades e seus híbridos.* Circulo Paulista de Orquidófilos. São Paulo, Brasil.

Machado, Érico de Freitas. 1981. Trinta anos como "mateiro" no paraíso das orquídeas. In *Orquidófilos E Orquidólogos,* pp. 47–58, Rio de Janeiro, Brasil.

McVaugh, Rogers. 1985. *Flora Novo-Galiciana,* Vol. 16 *Orchidaceae.* University of Michigan Press, Ann Arbor, MI.

Odebrecht, Sandra Altenburg. 1988. A trip to see orchids in Minas Gerais, Brazil. *Am. Orchid Soc. Bull.* 57 (10):1116–1120.

Pabst, Guido. 1984. The Section *Parviflorae* Lindl. of the genus *Laelia. Orchid Digest* 48 (1): 13–21, 24–32. This is the English translation by Stelzner and Duveen of Pabst's articles, Part IV (V?) of his below series, updated and annotated by Duveen and Fowlie.

Pabst, Guido and F. Dungs. 1974. Die Gattung *Laelia*, Teil I, Einführung. *Die Orchidee* 25:212–216. Teil II. Die Sektion *Cattleyodes* 25:256–262, 1975. Teil III/IV. Die Sektionen *Hadrolaelia* und *Microlaelia* 26: 157–162, 1975. Teil IV (should have been V). Die Sektion *Parviflorae*, 1 and 2, 29:156–165 and 296–200, 1978 (this part without F. Dungs as co-author).

Pabst, G. and F. Dungs. 1975, 1977. *Orchidaceae Brasilienses*. Vol. I and II. Brücke-Verlag Kurt Schmersow. Hildesheim.

Rolfe, R. A 1894. *Laelia tenebrosa*, Walton Grange variety. *Orchid Review* 2:15.

Rolfe, R. A 1896. *Laelia anceps* and its varieties. *Orchid Review* 4(38):50–53. See also Jan. 1922 issue for similar article.

Rose, James. 1986. *Laelia pumila*—a Brazilian adventure. *Am. Orchid Soc. Bull.* 55(10):988–995.

Royal Gardens, Kew. 1900. List of published names of plants introduced to cultivation: 1876–1896. *Bull. Misc. Information, Kew, additional series IV.*

Schlechter, R. 1917. Die Einteilung der Gattung *Laelia* und die geographische Verbreitung ihrer Gruppen. *Orchis* 11(5):87–96.

Stewart, Joyce. 1987. Early 'varieties' of *Laelia anceps*. *Am. Orchid Soc. Bull.* 56(5):492–498.

Urpía, Hernani. 1953. *Laelia grandis*, Ldl. *Am. Orchid Soc. Bull.* 22(1):6–11.

Urpía, Hernani. 1954. *Laelia lobata. Am. Orchid Soc. Bull.* 23(7):463–464.

Veitch, J. and Sons. 1887. *Laelia*. In *Manual of Orchidaceous Plants*. Chelsea.

Vuilleumier, Francois. 1988. Avian diversity in tropical ecosystems of South America and the design of national parks. *Biota Bulletin* 1 (2):5–33.

Withner, Carl L. 1977. Threatened and endangered species of orchids. In *Extinction is Forever*, eds. G. T. Prance and T. S. Elias, pp. 314–322. New York Botanical Garden, Bronx, New York.

Withner, Carl L. and H. Adams. 1960. Generic relationships and evolution among the cattleyas and their relatives. *Proceedings of the Third World Orchid Conference*. London.

Plant Name Index

Index of Persons

General Index